LIONEL
A Collector's Guide
and History

Volume III: Standard Gauge

Other Books and Videos
by Tom McComas and James Tuohy

Volumes in the Lionel Collector's Guide Series

Volume I: Prewar O Gauge
Volume II: Postwar
Volume III: Standard Gauge
Volume IV: 1970–1980
Volume V: The Archives
Volume VI: Advertising & Art

Lionel Price & Rarity Guides

Postwar 1945–1969, No. 1
Postwar 1945–1969, No. 2
Prewar 1900–1945
1970–1989
1970–1992

Books

Great Toy Train Layouts of America
Collecting Toy Trains

Videos

Lionel: The Movie
Great Layouts of America Series, Parts 1–6
Toy Train Revue Video Quarterly
The History of Lionel Trains
The Making of the Scale Hudson
Fun and Thrills with American Flyer
I Love Toy Trains
The New Lionel Showroom Layout
How to Build a Layout
Lionel Postwar
1991 Lionel Video Catalog
1992 Lionel Video Catalog

LIONEL

A Collector's Guide and History

Volume III: Standard Gauge

By Tom McComas & James Tuohy

HISTORY SECTION WITH RON HOLLANDER

PHOTOGRAPHY BY CHARLES OSGOOD, TOM McCOMAS, RON HOLLANDER & JOSEPH STEINMETZ

Chilton Book Company
Radnor, Pennsylvania

For Bill Vagell, with affection

CONTENTS

INTRODUCTION

Some details of the early years of the Lionel Corporation are a bit murky, as all experienced collectors probably know. Just when certain items were made cannot always be determined with absolute certainty. The procedure the authors used in determining manufacturing dates was quite simple: we went by the catalogs. But since the first catalog did not appear until 1903, and there are no catalogs available for 1907 and 1908, the dates that certain early pieces were made were determined by manufacturing techniques, most of which are explained in the course of the book.

As usual, we did not rely on our own knowledge alone in compiling information for this book. We had the help of literally hundreds of collectors across the country. Foremost among these was Carey Williams, whose youth proves that Standard gauge expertise is not limited to any one age group. Nor is it limited to any geographical area of the country. Carey, only 18, has spent almost his entire life in the scholarly pursuit of the train collecting hobby and he has successfully dispelled many misconceptions held by older generations about Standard gauge.

A very special thanks is also extended to David Christianson and Frank Petruzzo for information shared and guidance delivered, as well as to Jerry Williams, Don Renner and Victor Jendras.

The authors are deeply indebted, as they always are, to those patient and trusting collectors who allowed their trains to be photographed. These include Joseph Bak, Gary Baloun, David Christianson, Dave Garrigues, Howard Godel, Bob Hauser, Mike Hill, Charles Hinshaw, Peter Jugle, Joseph Kotil, John Kubis, John Monteverdi, Bob Morgan, Frank Petruzzo, Elliott Smith, Charles Wardwell, Thomas Spanic, and Carey Williams.

Others who helped include Hector Labarca, Michael Bookbinder, Carl Shaw and Lou Shur.

Finally the authors must mention the splendid craftsmen who have been responsible for the production of not just this book, but Volumes I and II.

We were fortunate to have worked with people of talent and pride, and even more fortunate that they were people of patience. These included Steve Boston, Jerry Hoffman, Joel Bolton and Al Leger of Boston Linotype, Evanston, Illinois, the typesetter; Gilbert Del Santo, John Avello, Wayne Alles and David Laurine of Studio Graphics, Chicago, Illinois, the lithographer; William Davidson of Davidson Litho, Chicago, Illinois, the printer.

Next to them all the authors were brash amateurs who were always asking dumb questions or making irritating requests. The re-setting of a paragraph here, the change of a color there, the moving of pictures and captions everywhere. They seldom complained and the books we feel, show how well pros can adjust to amateurs.

HISTORY

Much of the reporting and research for this history section was done by Ron Hollander, a New York City writer of considerable skill and a train collector of considerable knowledge.

There is a tendency, natural enough among younger collectors, to look upon the days at the turn of this century, when Lionel and other toy train companies were just starting out, as sort of the Dark Ages of train transportation, a time when everything in both the real and model railroading business was, well, a bit primitive.

It is true that Lionel's very first 2⅞-inch-gauge cars and some of the earliest Standard-gauge models have never threatened to take Best-of-Show at an industrial designers' convention, but it is also true that it was not long after that first effort that Lionel was making a number of high-quality and accurate reproductions. And Ives, of course, was a company that by 1900 was already making floor trains with such sophisticated clockwork mechanisms that they have never really been improved upon.

At the same time, the real railroads, although some decades away from streamliners and diesel power, were in some ways enjoying their best days. It was an exciting time.

The fast limited trains were being put into service at the end of the 19th Century, including the Pennsylvania's *Broadway Limited,* originally named the *Pennsylvania Limited,* and the New York Central's inspirationally named *Twentieth*

Century Limited. On June 11, 1905, the *Pennsylvania Limited,* operating on an 18-hour schedule between New York and Chicago and pulled by a 4-4-0 D-16-type loco, reached a speed of 127.1 miles an hour.

Other trains of the era were not merely plugging along either. The New York Central turned out an engine it wanted to display at the 1893 Columbian Exposition in Chicago, which was that year's World Fair. It was named the *999,* and on May 10, 1893, heading the *Empire State Express* between Syracuse and Buffalo, drove for a mile at the rate of 112.5 miles an hour. Nothing up until that time, and few things since, ever rolled on rails as fast.

These accomplishments in speed did not go unnoticed. Press agentry, often considered a product of a more modern era, was noisily alive in the 1890s, especially on the New York Central in the person of George Henry Daniels. Daniels was a short, energetic man who had a white goatee and is considered by many as the greatest railroad publicity man of the last 100 years.

It was Daniels who had the biggest hand in naming both the *Empire State Express* and the *Twentieth Century Limited.* He was also the

4-4-0 Empire State Express

man who suggested that a fast new loco, the *999,* be built just for the purpose of publicizing the new *Empire State Express* and that it be built in time to be shown off at the Columbian Exposition. That wasn't all he did to get publicity for the new express. After the newspapers gave great play to the miraculous 112-mile-an-hour-mile figure, he did a sales job on the postmaster general of the United States and shortly thereafter the Post Office came out with a new two-cent stamp. Pictured in two colors on the stamp was the *Empire State Express.* Advertising and publicity men still like to talk about that one.

The *999* was a 4-4-0 and was not all that dissimilar to some of the early model trains being turned out by American toymakers, especially a 2-inch gauge 4-4-0 made by Howard in 1906 and Lionel's number 6 of 1908.

One railroading event that took place at the Turn of the Century remains memorialized forever, it seems, by a song. On April 30, 1900, about the time young Joshua Lionel Cowen was trying to start his toy train company, a man named John Luther Jones, an engineer on the Illinois Central, ran his speeding freight into the rear of an improperly side-tracked caboose near Vaughn, Miss., causing a mighty wreck and killing Jones, who was known as Casey. The event itself went relatively unnoticed and would have remained that way except for Wallace Saunders, a worker in the Illinois Central roundhouse at Canton, Mississippi. Saunders liked to sing songs and to compose

them, too. Saunders knew Jones and often worked on his engine and soon after Jones was killed Saunders was singing the song that was to become an immortal of the rails, although it underwent quite a bit of changes before it was published in 1903 as *Casey Jones, the Brave Engineer,* words by T. Lawrence Siebert and music by Eddie Newton.

By 1903, Joshua Lionel Cowen had teamed up with Harry Grant and had started the Lionel Mfg. Company. Grant was an able man who many experts believe was instrumental in the early success of Lionel, having more mechanical expertise than Cowen. Grant developed the motor which was used in the 300 electric trolley car, which came out in 1902 in 2⅞-inch gauge. The trolley bodies were actually made by the Converse Company and no one is sure whether they were delivered to Lionel already painted, whether Lionel had Converse paint them to order, or if Lionel painted the cars itself. Since there were only two people working at Lionel at the time — Cowen and Grant — it seems unlikely they painted them. But it is also quite possible they ordered what they wanted painted on the trolley. It said "City Hall Park" on one side and "Union Depot" on the other. City Hall Park in New York is across the street from City Hall in Manhattan, about four blocks away from 24 Murray Street, where the first Lionel office and plant was. This suggests that Cowen or Grant, familiar as they were with the City Hall Park trolley, ordered the paint job.

Grant stayed with Lionel until 1910, and was the plant superintendent. Then, amid rumors of a falling out with Cowen, he left the company when it moved to New Haven. Although the circumstances of why Harry Grant left Lionel are unclear, what is clear is that he was replaced by a good man, Mario Caruso. Mario and his brother, Victor, were Italian immigrants who started as solderers for Lionel in 1910. Through the years they were responsible for a number of patents, just as Grant had been in the earlier years. Mario Caruso would become works manager and finally secretary-treasurer of Lionel. He retired in 1945.

One of Caruso's inventions was the "automatic" coupler Lionel brought out in 1923. "Automatic" was Lionel's name for the coupler, but it was far from that. Collectors most often refer to the coupler as the latch, or Caruso, coupler. What Caruso was seeking was a coupler that would hook together cars without lifting them off the track. He succeeded in doing that, but it was still extremely difficult to couple cars in less than three or four tries.

By 1924, Lionel's sales figures had surpassed those of Ives, the older and much revered toy company that had begun manufacturing electric trains in 1910. For the first time Lionel sales exceeded Ives and Lionel became the number-one toy train maker in the country.

The year 1924 was when a young stock boy joined Lionel. His name was Frank Pettit and he would become a prolific inventor and eventually manager of the products development department. Along the way Pettit married Mario Caruso's niece and kept the coupler patent in the family, so to speak, by inventing the remote-control electric coupler, the patent of which is dated October 21, 1938.

Pettit also invented the merchandise car and the barrel and log unloading cars, but that was a long time after 1924, when Pettit was starting out in the company. In his early days Pettit functioned as an odd-job man, sometimes chauffeuring Joshua Cowen between the company offices on 21st Street in New York City and the factory, which spread across the city limits of Irvington and Hillside, New Jersey.

"He would call me 'boy'," says Pettit, now a handsome white-haired man who still invents things, although not for toy trains. "He'd have me do projects at his home, like make a telephone table or a kitchen cabinet."

Pettit was hired by Arthur Raphael, the brilliant merchandiser who was Cowen's right hand man, sales manager and, by 1940, executive vice president and a member of the board of directors.

"Raphael liked to have only college students working for him," says Pettit. "Now, I wasn't going to college, but when Raphael asked if I were, I said, 'Yes, sir.'

" 'What are you studying?' Raphael asked me.

" 'Dentistry,' I lied.

" 'Dentistry!' Raphael says, looking at me. 'You aren't tall enough to reach the patient.'

" 'Still,' I said, 'I'm studying dentistry.'

" 'Okay,' Raphael says, 'You're hired.' "

That first Christmas, Pettit worked in the stock room with a messenger named Vivian, who apparently was the best dressed messenger boy in New York City. Vivian had the same, short, stumpy build as the big boss, Joshua Cowen, and Cowen, an expensive dresser, would give Vivian beautifully tailored, hand-me-down suits.

"From the back Vivian would look just like Cowen," says Pettit.

Cowen was always clothes-conscious and even after he had retired and was living in Florida in the 1960s, he continued to buy suits that were hand-tailored.

"Mr. Cowen was not concerned about price," says Allen Zwick, a tailor who fitted Cowen often in the later years of his life. "What he wanted was good material — his taste ran to conservative grays, blues and browns — and a good fit. He'd often buy five suits at a time."

Zwick, who now runs a fashionable clothing store on the North Shore of Chicago, once had a conversation with Cowen about a man named William F. Allen. Zwick had seen a plaque in the waiting room of the Union Station in Washington to the memory of William F. Allen, and Zwick asked Cowen if he knew anything about Allen.

3

"It's funny you should ask that," answered Cowen. "I once thought about naming a Lionel passenger car after Allen, but I never did get around to it."

It turns out that Allen, although most people don't realize it, had a great deal to do with how Americans keep time. For it was William Allen who devised the plan for dividing the United States into four time zones. He did it at the urging of the railroads, who by the 1870s realized the need of standardizing time in this country.

Most people are of the idea that time zones were invented by someone like Benjamin Franklin or Thomas Jefferson back in the first days of the republic. But that is not correct. Time in the United States, until the railroads and William Allen came along, was pretty much a local matter. Generally speaking, each of the larger cities had its own local time, regulated by the sun, which was adopted by most — but not always by all — of the smaller towns in the region. This meant that time not only was off by hours, depending on where you were in the country, but by minutes as well. For instance, in 1880 when solar time was noon in Chicago, it was 12:31 in Pittsburgh, 12:24 in Cleveland, 12:13 in Cincinnati, 12:09 in Louisville, 12:07 in Indianapolis, 11:50 in St. Louis, 11:48 in Dubuque, 11:41 in St. Paul, and 11:27 in Omaha. According to Carlton J. Corliss, who wrote a pamphlet called *The Day of Two Noons,* there were at least 23 local times in Indiana, 27 in both Illinois and Michigan, and 38 in Wisconsin.

Until the coming of fast steam trains, these discrepancies meant relatively little, since travelers could not go far enough in one day to have the differences in time seriously affect them. But when trains ran faster and longer there was an increasing desire on the part of the railroads to devise some sort of time standardization.

The railroads formed a permanent organization which became successively the Time-Table Convention, the General Time Convention, the American Railway Association, and now the Association of American Railroads. On October 11, 1883, the first General Time Convention adopted the time zone plan developed by William Allen, a former resident engineer of the Camden & Amboy Railroad and secretary of the time convention.

The Allen plan called for five time zones — Intercolonial, Eastern, Central, Mountain, and Pacific, with the four United States time zones based on the 75th, 90th, 105th and 120th meridians west of Greenwich. The four American time belts are approximately on the longitudes of Philadelphia, Memphis, Denver and Fresno.

The railroads put their new time zone plan into effect on November 18, 1883, and soon almost all cities and towns adopted their times to railroad time, although the United States government did not for quite a while. Finally, on March 19, 1918, the Congress passed the Standard Time Act, which gave federal sanction to the four-zone system adopted by the railroads 35 years before.

History books don't usually mention the adoption of standard time in the United States, nor do they mention William F. Allen, who died in 1915. But the standarization of time was an important event in the nation's history nevertheless, and William Allen was a man who deserves to be remembered.

In 1931, after Lionel had taken over Ives, the firm's financial records were quite disorganized.

"Their accounting was horrible, no decent system at all," says Edward Zier, then a Price Waterhouse auditor who had been sent over to Lionel to put their books in order. "The company had just grown with no order to it."

Zier improved the bookkeeping system, although Zier remembers that Cowen, a man with many conflicting aspects to his personality, was rather wary of the work Zier, an outsider, was doing. "Here was a guy coming in and changing his world around," says Zier. But on the other hand Cowen could see the need for restructuring.

"This is like having an automobile and not knowing how to use it," he told Zier, and in the end Cowen offered Zier a job as the company's accountant and by 1946 he was elected comptroller of Lionel.

"Later Cowen said the best thing he ever did was to bring in professionals specifically trained for their jobs, rather than simply promoting whoever was there," Zier says. "He was pleased he brought in people like Joseph Bonnano, chief engineer, Joe Hanson, advertising manager, and myself in finance."

Zier says he believes Lionel was the first toy company to be on the Big Board of the New York Stock Exchange. Cowen, Zier and other company executives, excited as kids with a new choo-choo train, went down to Wall Street to watch, the first day the company's name was posted.

Cowen, sporadically but not infrequently, was moved to take his executives out of the offices, especially on warm summer afternoons.

"Hey, it's a beautiful day," Cowen would say suddenly. "What are we doing in here? Come on. Let's go up to the stadium."

And they would be off to Yankee Stadium to watch baseball, which Cowen loved. There was only one thing wrong with those idyllic afternoons. "To tell the truth," Zier says, "after the game we'd often go back to the office and work."

Cowen's lazy-afternoon policy was reflected by Arthur Raphael, who was in charge of sales, including the salesmen who staffed the Lionel showroom. William Gaston, a former Lionel salesman, says Raphael would walk into a showroom on a nice day and say, "There're eight of you here. Here's ten bucks. Four of you go up to the ball game today. The other four can go tomorrow."

Although there was not necessarily a connection between Cowen's love of baseball and his advertising policy, he did hire both Yankee great Joe DiMaggio and, later, Brooklyn Dodger star catcher Roy Campanella to do endorsements for Lionel trains. As ads go, the DiMaggio and Campanella endorsements were genuine. Both men had Lionel trains. Campanella, in fact, was interviewed in his home in the 1950s by Edward R. Murrow, the host of the television show, "Person-to-Person." In Campanella's basement was a large O gauge layout.

As the company grew and more supervisory jobs were necessary, Joshua Cowen relegated more responsibility, but he still involved himself in all aspects of the business (or would, as one executive said rather bitterly, "Stick his nose into things, interfere with production.") William K. Walthers, who founded the Walthers Modeling Company, called on Lionel one day in 1929.

"I asked them why they did not paint their toy signals in railroad colors (black and white) instead of a gaudy combination of colors that had no resemblance to real signals," says Walthers. "Mr. Cowen . . . came out of his inner office to answer my question.

"He said: 'Young man, do you know who actually buys toy trains and accessories? It's the women — mothers, sisters and aunts of the kids who play with them. Don't forget, women buy on color and they don't give a damn what the thing is, just as long as it is bright. How many signals do you think we would sell if they were painted black and white?' "

One of the early jobs of Frank Pettit, the odd-job man turned inventor, was to mix the actual test shades for those bright colors that Cowen liked so much.

"They had a color consultant come in — Howard Ketchum," says Pettit. "I was his assistant. Ketchum would bring in small cans of paint and say what colors he'd like and I'd mix them. I had a small paint-spray booth.

"There was no thought of prototype or realism. It had to appeal to the eye, that was all. We'd take off the journal boxes and I'd change them from nickel to copper. Or we'd try painting the journal yellow. The combinations would be all laid out, a choice would be made, and the factory would make a production model."

Pettit later was in charge of service repairs in the rear of the New York showroom, before the Lionel museum was started. "We had these two empty showcases in the showroom," Pettit says. "So I started putting old locomotives and cars in them. Customers would bring in old stuff and they'd be allowed 10 per cent off the new list price.

"We were taking in so much old stuff, who could use it all? Trolleys, cars, early numbers, 2⅞-inch gauge — everything. We couldn't keep it all, even with the showcases, so a lot of it got thrown out. God, what we threw out!" When he talks about those days Pettit gets that distant stare that collectors get when they tell "If only . . ." stories. He shrugs.

"Ah, who knew then what it would be worth."

Eventually the models that were saved went into the Lionel museum, which was administered by Irving Shull, who succeeded Pettit as head of service. Pettit and Schull had gone to school together and Pettit brought Schull into the company. After Pettit invented the automatic coupler, he was put in charge of Lionel's Preliminary model shop, which is where new ideas were tried out.

That preliminary model shop, apparently, was a top-secret area within the Lionel factory itself. Pettit, working alone, tried to keep all new creations to himself until they were completed, or at least he was sure they were feasible.

"Even the boss had to knock to get in," Pettit says proudly.

Cowen might have had to knock to get into the preliminary model shop, but he was liable to be, at any time and without knocking, anywhere else in the corporate offices or the factory.

There is a story that one day Cowen was driving along the Hudson and heard a New York Central passenger train emit a blast to signal a control tower. Cowen dashed back to the office.

"Men, the New York Central's got a new whistle," he announced in the engineering department, looking, as he was once described, like an anxious cherub. "It's a knockout. The finest thing I've heard in 40 years. We've got to have it. Drop everything else for the time being."

Cowen then set up shop for days with 12 men along the tracks near Harmon, trying to recreate the new whistle sound.

Cowen also could be fastidious to the point of distraction.

"He was very fussy," says Zier. "If someone left a book in the showroom where it didn't belong, it upset his sense of decorum. If his wife didn't read the Sunday paper fast enough, out it went. He had a mania about order and waste. He hated lights on that weren't necessary. He'd be a good man on the Energy Commission today. He'd kick up a storm, going around and turning out bulbs.

"He could flare up in an instant. One time I came by and he was shouting — storming — over nothing. I said to him, 'Sit down!'

" 'What?' he says to me.

" 'Sit down. You know what's going to happen to you? You'll have a heart attack, that's what.' "

Cowen sat down. Most Lionel employees recall his frequent outbursts as relatively inconsequential. His general relations with the workers seemed good. Bill Vagell, for years the biggest Lionel dealer on the East Coast, often visited the Irvington factory, coming from nearby Garfield, where Vagell ran the Treasure House Hobby Shop.

"Cowen was enthusiastic about everything that came out of that factory." Vagell says. "He was proud if it. He would go around patting people on the back. I've seen him pat women on the assembly line on the back because they worked so fast. He took a paternalistic interest in his employees."

Zier agrees. "Many employees did feel he was their father. I used to call him 'Pop,' especially in the later years. If you went to him with a personal problem, needing money, he wouldn't loan it to you, he'd grab the bill himself."

Cowen was liberal with Christmas bonuses, too. Salesman William Gaston received a $100 bonus in Christmas of 1947, barely a year after he started.

"At my last place they had given me ten bucks and I was happy," Gaston says. Later, when Gaston's wife had a baby, he received another $100, plus a blanket from Cowen and a bassinet from Raphael.

Cowen also gave out elaborate gifts to other employees and buyers: Cartier wallets, crystal cigaret boxes, gold lighters. One Christmas Zier came across Cowen wrapping some presents for the buyers himself, giving them to the office women to mail.

"You must be the most expensive office boy in the country," Zier said to Cowen, who did not smile.

"He didn't like that," says Zier, "and he held a mild grudge against me for awhile for saying it."

Cowen, on the other hand, was a difficult man to buy a present for. His son, Larry, said Cowen once received 29 presents for Christmas and returned 28 of them.

"Once I got him a pair of cufflinks," says Zier. "They were expensive by my standards. He said he loved them, but a week later he brought them back to the store."

One day, when Gaston was doing floor duty in the Lionel showroom, a retarded little boy who had difficulty talking said he would like to have an electric train. The child was standing at the railing of the layout. Just then "J. L.," as he was known to the salesmen, walked into the room.

"Bill, get this kid's address," said Cowen. Gaston got the address and the boy and his mother left. Cowen took the slip of paper with the address on it to another salesman.

"Here, go out to their house," Cowen said. "See what kind of family it is. See if they're poor. If they are, give 'em a train set."

Gaston, recalling the incident, says, "But you see, he wanted them checked out first."

Cowen was never completely without suspicion. Gaston was sitting in the showroom one day with his back to the main door. Cowen came marching through from the executive offices.

"Turn around," he told Gaston. "You sit with your back to the door and some guy will come in here and steal something."

"And you know," Gaston adds now, "damned if somebody didn't. Stole a handmade sample of the electronic ore car. You should have heard Cowen. You'd think the world came to an end."

Showroom duty was considered a chore by the Lionel salesmen. They would spend most of their time on the road, but every salesman had to spend a certain amount of time at the home office, working the showroom floor, answering questions from children and generally being bored. Sometimes they would liven things up a bit. Many of the salesmen, after World War II, were veterans. One day they dragged the big fans in the showroom in a line, like motors on a bomber.

"Then we lined up the chairs, two in front of the fans, one toward the back, and so forth," says Gaston. "We started rocking back and forth, sitting in the chairs, calling out to each other, 'Pilot to tail gunner, pilot to tail gunner, milk cars at four o'clock. Coming in fast . . . Rrrr!' "

On other occasions, when things were slow around the showroom, the salesmen would race several trains on the layout towards the same crossover. This might result in several collisions a day. Finally Cowen had the crossovers made collision proof.

"Another time," says Gaston, "when we were carrying the line of fishing tackle, we used to tie a ball to the end of a rod and try casting it into a cup. We were doing this when we hit the overhead sprinkler system one day and down came the water. The showroom floor was full of water. The firemen came up and everything."

Things weren't always slow in the showroom, and kids were not the only people who were around. One day in 1948 when there was quite a crowd in the showroom, Gaston walked into the stock room and saw Frank Sinatra. He was buying a set for someone and Gaston, realizing the singer would get mobbed by the crowd out front, suggested he and his bodyguard take the back elevator, where they could get out through a door which exited on 27th Street. Sinatra thanked Gaston and took the suggestion.

7

Sinatra, incidentally, has retained an interest in toy trains through the years and has a collection at his Palm Springs, California, home.

Another time there was a big crowd in the showroom was when Roy Campanella, confined to a wheel chair after his paralyzing automobile accident, threw a special switch that started all the new trains running on the layout.

Ezio Pinza was a frequent visitor in the Lionel showroom, as was Evelyn, of "Evelyn and Her Magic Violin" fame.

That all merely demonstrates that all kinds of people retained an interest in toy trains into their adult years, if such a demonstration were needed. Robert Montgomery, the actor, had a layout in his elegant Hollywood home, and he had holes punched in the walls so the trains could travel from room to room. Ben Hecht, the writer, specialized in wrecks. He liked to crash the trains, then bring up a wrecker and restore order without ever using his hands to place cars back on the tracks.

Even Dr. James Conant, the intellectual president of Harvard in the 1940s, had a layout on the ballroom floor of the university's presidential mansion.

On an autumn afternoon in the early 1950s a short well-dressed man with a thin mustache entered the showroom, walked over to Gaston and asked to see Joshua Cowen. Gaston said, "See the receptionist." He later found out the man was Walt Disney.

In those postwar days, Frank Pettit was very busy in the privacy of his preliminary model room. He designed more than 150 items and those he holds the patent on include, besides the automatic coupler, the merchandise car, the barrel unloader, the log loader, the knuckle coupler, and the barrel car.

Many of Pettit's designs were never marketed, including: a caboose with an operating flagman at its rear, a plywood unloading platform with operating car, a magazine-fed mail bag pickup car, and an oil-filling bulk oil station with a pipe that pumped liquid into a tank car. This last item operated along the lines of the 38 water tower.

Pettit also had designs for an all-plastic bascule bridge, an overhead freight crane, and a freight platform with a freight unloading derrick on one corner of it.

Pettit still has working models of items that were put into production, and some that were not. He has the first working animated newsstand which he made by hand. The newsstand is orange and there are scraps of tiny newspapers pasted overhead. An oversized man, rather crudely painted, is reading a newspaper which Pettit made by cutting down a real paper.

"I showed it to Cowen," Pettit says, "and he said to go ahead with it. The hydrant and the dog were then added.

He also has a working model of an articulated, six-wheel drive loco, which was never produced, and a trackside billboard which was made up of horizontal strips. The billboard shows a Baby Ruth ad, and as the train passes, the billboard strips flip, making a different ad on their backs. There is also a working model of an unproduced operating crane with an extendable boom, big enough to raise cars. Ben Hecht would have loved it.

After an item was designed by Pettit or others in the engineering department and a brass or wood mockup made, there would be a point at which it was introduced to the salesmen.

"You'd come into the sales meeting room and you'd see all the new items lined up," says Gaston. "Joe Bonnano would show us how the things worked. Sometimes we'd say if something seemed impractical, like the 38 water tower with water in it. A kid could knock it over and the water would spill out.

"They'd tell us what price they were putting on it. We might say, 'Nah, that won't go for 11 dollars. It should be 9.'

"I remember they showed us the Southern F-3 and they were going to bring it out in blue and white, the freight colors.

" 'That's the wrong color, Mr. Ginsburg,' I said. (Allen Ginsburg took over as sales manager after Arthur Raphael retired.) 'You bring

213 lift bridge prototype, never manufactured. O gauge, originally from collection of Louis Napoliello of New Jersey, now owned by Bob Hauser and Joe Ranker of New Jersey. Bridge, along with other prototypes, were "just lying around" when Lionel Irvington plant was closed in 1966, and various employees who were interested just "took them home with them."

that out in blue and you'll be the laughing stock.'

" 'Well,' said Ginsburg, 'do you know somebody down there with Southern?'

"So I got them the specs from Southern and of course it came out in green. Green was for passenger and was the more common Southern color."

The railroads readily supplied Lionel and the other toy companies with their specifications and also a list of names of their passenger cars. Lionel could then select any names they wanted.

Lionel never gave any specific names to their low-priced Pullman cars, just using the word "Pullman" on the sides of the cars. In a way, it's too bad Lionel did not use any of the names that the Pullman Company gave their cars, because some of them — a group named from Greek and Roman mythology — were among the most colorful ever to appear on the railroads.

Among Pullman porters there grew a legend that those wonderful names were thought up by Florence Pullman, daughter of the founder of the company, who received $100 for each name she selected. But that legend was officially denied by the company. What had happened was that Pullman acquired the Wagner Palace Car Company, its chief competitor, and discovered that 300 Wagner names duplicated names already being used by Pullman. The names had to be changed quickly.

A Pullman vice president then took a group of clerks over to the Chicago Public Library where they scoured Greek and Roman mythology books and within 24 hours came up with 300 marvelous off-beat names, ranging from *Circe* and *Sibyl* to *Archimedes* and *Belisarius*.

So that's the way the cars were really named and the legend of Florence Pullman turned out to be untrue, and that is kind of sad. For, as

Stewart H. Holbrook, a great writer of informal history, said in his book, *The Story of American Railroads:*

"I for one prefer to think of Miss Florence Pullman, a copy of Shelley in one hand, gazing out the window at the glistening waters of Lake Michigan, a faraway look in her eyes, earning an honest dollar by applying the name of some Aegean god to a new car that is waiting, shining yet nameless, on the factory sidetracks in Pullman, Illinois."

*   *   *   *   *

The early post-World War II years saw Lionel enjoying its greatest boom. From the late 1940s through the mid-1950s Lionel could barely make enough trains.

"It was a sellers' market," says former salesman Gaston. "You might get an order for, say, 60 pair of switches. 'You can't have that,' the salesman would say. 'I'll give you 48.'"

And even then, Gaston would know the factory would cut the order back some more.

Everything was going right for Lionel, which had the postwar O-gauge market to itself. An independent survey in 1950 showed that Lionel's catalog ranked right behind Sears and Ward's in public acceptance.

But of course it did not last, for reasons that have been thoroughly chronicled elsewhere in this book, as well as the authors' other works on Lionel. O-gauge toy trains were quietly passing from the scene by the 1960s, just as many real trains were, just as the stagecoach had 100 years before that, and airplanes might 100 years from now. With the passing of each mode of transportation it seems an irreplaceable part of our heritage is lost, but then it always seems it is replaced.

There was a poem written in the 19th Century by Peter Wells of Jervis, New York, mourning the passing of the stagecoach. It ended like this:

> *O, that was music! when at morn*
> *As, winding around by yon old hill,*
> *The driver blew his sounding horn,*
> *And echo answered from the hill.*
> *No echoing horn and prancing team.*
> *Is heard amid this age of steam.*
> *But drawn beneath some sheltering shed*
> *The old stagecoach neglected stands;*
> *Its curtains flapping in the wind—*
> *The ghost of ruin's waving hands:*
> *While on the wheels the gathering rust*
> *Proclaims the mortal "dust to dust."*
> *While in the field their scattered bones,*
> *Or on the common turned to die:*
> *Their trips all o'er—their routes all run—*
> *The driver's pride and labor gone,*
> *And he like one who stands alone.*

That was written about the stagecoach, but it could have been written about the steam engine, or perhaps the propeller airplane or the Apollo rocket or the space shuttle.

They all might pass, but happily, there will always be the toys.

2 7/8-INCH GAUGE

1901-1905

The first trains made by Lionel were called 2⅞-inch gauge because the distance between the rails measured 2⅞ inches.

The dictionary defines the word "rare" as "thinly scattered, not massed." We have used the word many times in our books and will use it in this section, too. However, there are no trains we have talked about or will ever talk about that are as thinly scattered and unmassed as Lionel's 2⅞-inch-gauge trains.

In all there are about 30 collectable versions, including trailers and color variations. The largest known 2⅞-gauge collection has a total of seven pieces. For items like the derrick and green 100 loco there are only three or four known. In fact, the only original 2⅞-inch piece we were able to find to photograph for this book is shown on the next page. All the others are reproductions. The Converse trolley is from the collection of Charles Wardwell. All the black and white photographs are of reproductions made in the mid-fifties by the McCoy Manufacturing Co. of Kent, Washington. A total of 100 units were made and about 50 of the 100 units were cranes. The other 50 units McCoy made were divided between the gondola, "jail car" and the B&O No. 5. Even these reproductions are highly prized. James Cohen of Trumball, Connecticut, is currently making 2⅞-inch-gauge reproductions.

Because of this extreme rarity few collectors know, or even care, about 2⅞-inch trains. The chances of finding a 2⅞-inch-gauge item in the "field" are remote. But it wasn't always that way. In the late fifties a Midwestern collector discovered six different 2⅞-inch-gauge pieces at a garage sale. He bought them all for three dollars — 50 cents apiece, which was the asking price. It was one of the few times in history when a train collector did not try to buy trains for lower than the asking price.

The first 2⅞-inch trains were made in 1901, when production runs were very small. Joshua Cowen operated only about six months out of the year in the beginning, closing down during slow periods and not reopening until enough orders accumulated to justify going into production again. Often he would open at a different location. That is why Lionel had so many different addresses in those early years.

The 2⅞-inch trains were made through 1905. With the exception of the 100 loco, they all came with motorless trailers. Trailers are harder to find than motorized units but they do not command a higher price because a trailer is simply a locomotive with the motor removed. No catalog numbers were stamped on the 2⅞-inch gauge trains.

All 2⅞-inch-gauge locos used the same type of electric motor and were either powered by batteries or direct current. Track had to be assembled. Each strip section was about 12-inches long and had to be inserted into grooves on the wood ties. Frames were cast iron and the trucks were sprung. Some early bodies were made from wood but most other 2⅞-inch trains were stamped from sheet metal. All the locos had a manual reverse and the early bodies were painted apple green and later units were usually maroon.

We cover 2⅞-inch-gauge in this book only to give our readers the complete history of trains made by Lionel. A new collector should definitely not try to collect 2⅞-inch. He'd be better off searching for the Loch Ness Monster. When 2⅞-inch pieces do change hands, they pass from one established collector to another.

100 "B&O NO. 5" ELECTRIC LOCO
1903-1905

This piece was modeled after a tunnel loco of the B&O Railroad. Collectors call it the B&O No. 5 because that is what is rubber-stamped on the sides. It is most often found painted maroon with a black roof and base. An apple green version is extremely rare — only four are known to exist. This was the only 2⅞-inch loco that did not come with a trailer.

200 ELECTRIC EXPRESS
1901-1905

This was a small motorized gondola. The first versions were made of wood and were lettered "Electric Express." Early wood gondolas did not have brass corners. Later wood gondolas had brass corners. Later, the gondola body was made of stamped sheet metal. The metal version came in apple green or maroon. "Lake Shore" was rubber stamped on the sides. A rare variation is known stamped "B&O." A 400 trailer car was also made in sheet metal and is known to exist in both apple green and maroon.

The later metal gondola is the 2⅞-inch-gauge piece that turns up most often. Any early wood gondola is extremely rare.

300 CONVERSE TROLLEY
1902-1905

Morton E. Converse and Company was a firm that was making floor toys at the same time Lionel started making electric trains. Lionel bought Converse trolley bodies and added a frame with a motor. Like all trolleys, these are highly prized by collectors. Its prototype was the summer trolley that was a familiar sight in big cities at the time. The Converse body was rather flimsy and was easily damaged. A 309 trolley trailer was made, too.

The early trolleys had brass wheels and no coupler pocket. Later trolleys had cast wheels and a coupler pocket was added. The trolleys were painted maroon and apple green. No one is sure whether Converse sold the bodies to Lionel already painted or if Lionel painted them. They came equipped with a destination board lettered "City Hall Park" on one side and "Union Depot" on the reverse side.

The Converse trolley is very hard to find in good condition and the trailer is even harder to find. The trailer is known to exist with the later cast wheels only.

500 MOTORIZED DERRICK
1903-1904

This piece featured a manually operated derrick that was secured to a metal base. The base was attached to a motorized cast frame. Early cranes were light green and later ones

were painted maroon. A 600 derrick trailer was also made and came in the same two colors as the motorized version.

The apple green derrick is more "thinly scattered" and less "massed" than any other 2⅞-inch-gauge piece. Three are known to exist.

800 BOX CAR
1904-1905

This car is referred to as the "jail car" because it has bars on the windows. "Metropolitan Express" is rubber-stamped on the sides and it is known to exist only in painted maroon with a black roof and frame. A matching 900 trailer was also made.

The "jail car" is one of the more common 2⅞-inch-gauge pieces.

1000 PASSENGER CAR
1905

This was the last 2⅞-inch train Lionel made. It resembled a trolley or day coach and was painted maroon with a black roof and frame. It came with a number of different names rubber-stamped on the sides. Some names that are known include "Metropolitan Express," "Maryland St. Ry. Co." and "Metropolitan St. R. R. Co."

Both the 1000 passenger car and the 1050 trailer are usually found in poor condition. They are very flimsy compared to the other 2⅞-inch pieces.

RATING

The derrick and wooden gondola are the two 2⅞-inch pieces that have proven to be the hardest to find. Only three derricks and four wood gondolas are known to exist. Next would be the 1000 passenger in top condition. All the other pieces are about equal in scarcity. The late gondola and jail car turn up the most often.

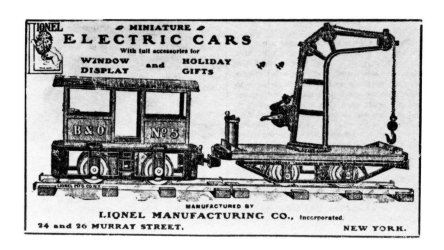

1903 Lionel catalog.

EARLY PERIOD

STEAMERS

Lionel's early steamers were modeled after yard switchers that were common on the East coast at the turn of the century. Lionel's locos had a great deal of charm and they appeal to both train collectors and toy collectors.

The steamers were first cataloged in 1906 and last cataloged in 1926. Their basic appearance, as well as the methods used to construct them, remained pretty much the same through their entire run. They were made of stamped sheet metal. Boilers were "Russian blue metal" — made from the same process used in making gun barrels — and wood. Pilots and window trim were painted red and lettering was rubber-stamped in gold. Road names included N.Y.C. & H.R.R. (New York Central & Hudson River Railroad, also appears as N.Y.C. & H.R.R.R.), Pennsylvania Railroad, B. & O., and P. & L. E.R.R. (Pittsburgh & Lake Erie Railroad). The last two are the hardest to find. N.Y.C. & H.R.R. is the most common. Some higher

priced locos were made in brass and nickel. These brass locos had no lettering. There are many variations in lettering. Almost every year, when rubber stamps wore out, they were replaced by stamps with a different typeface.

6 Tender pre-production model with Pittsburg & Lake Erie markings.

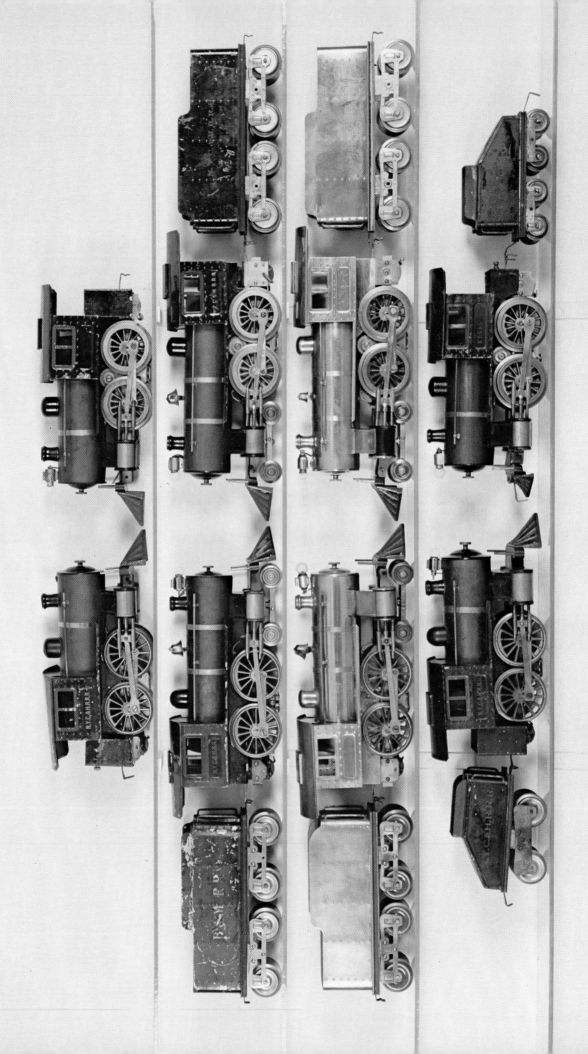

Although basic appearance did not change, there are ways to pinpoint when a loco was made. The earliest locos had drivers with a thin rim, a split frame, dummy headlight and drum reverse. The earliest tenders had a short, straight coupler and either solid or open three-rivet trucks. Locos with these early characteristics are the most sought-after of all the Early-period locos.

1st 10 series truck — solid 3 rivet.

2nd 10 series truck — open 3 rivet.

In 1908 Lionel introduced an operating headlight for the first time. Trains made by the Howard Miniature Lamp Company had featured a working headlight since 1904. Added in 1911 was a terminal used to illuminate passenger cars. A wire would run from the last car through the other cars and connect to the terminal on the locomotive. This terminal was placed on the rear of the 5 and inside the cab on the 6.

Car lighting terminal with 27 Lighting Set for cars.

THIN-RIM VERSIONS
5
6 — open three-rivet trucks on tender
7 — open three-rivet trucks on tender
5 Special — solid three-rivet trucks on tender

The split frame was dropped and the solid frame adopted in 1911. Thick-rimmed drivers replaced the more realistic looking thin-rimmed drivers in 1912. That same year the pedestal headlight replaced the slide-on type.

Early split frame.

Later solid frame.

All early steamers had hand reverse levers and were painted black with the exception of the brass locos. Numbers appeared in the catalog only, never on the locos. In the photo on the opposite page we show the four Early period steamers in both their thin and thick-rimmed versions.

Thin-rim 5.

5
0-4-0
1906-1926

The 5 first appeared in the 1906 catalog. It remained available, in one way or another, through 1926. It was the smallest and lowest priced of all the Early period steamers and was

designed to go with the medium or large passenger cars and 10 series freights.

The earliest 5s had a split frame, dummy headlight, thin-rimmed drivers and no tender. This same early version also came with a four-wheel sloped-back tender and the tender had a single 10 series truck. It was given the catalog designation of 5 Special. This four-wheel tender is very rare and came with both the solid three-rivet truck and open three-rivet truck. The solid three-rivet truck was earlier and therefore more desirable.

5 Special tender with solid 3-rivet trucks.

About 1910 the 5 Special came with an eight-wheel sloped-back tender which had two 100-series trucks. This same 5 Special was shown in the 1912 catalog but with the designation 51.

So the same basic loco was referred to in various catalogs as the 5, 5 Special and 51, the only difference being the tender. The 5 and 5 Special had a large coal bunker. The 51 had a smaller coal bunker.

Of all the 5s, the earliest version with the four-wheel tender and lettered B&O is the most sought after. Next would be any early 5 with thin-rimmed drivers, split frame and a four-wheel tender. Later 5s with thick-rimmed drivers, solid frames and eight-wheel tenders are the most common of the early steamers.

6 with thin rims.

6, 6 SPECIAL, 7
4-4-0
1906-1923

The 6 was the biggest loco Lionel made at the time and was designed to match the biggest and best locos of the competition. It first appeared in the 1906 catalog and ran through 1923. The 6 was nicely proportioned and has an appealing toy choo-choo look. It went with the large passenger cars and 10 series freights. The eight-wheel rectangular tender came with two 10-series trucks.

Thin-rim 7 above and in color
on opposite page.

The 6 Special was for those who wanted an unusual loco and were willing to pay for it. It was the same loco as the 6 but was made of brass and nickel and sold for twice as much as the regular version. It was made in 1908 and 1909 and came with a split frame and thin-rimmed drivers. Its tender had open three-rivet trucks.

In 1910 the number of the 6 Special was changed to 7, and it kept that designation every year through 1923, when it was discontinued. It had thin rims through 1911, but every year thereafter had thick rims.

Lionel showed a six-wheel drive steam loco in the 1907 catalog with the number designation 7. It is not known to exist nor is any other six-wheel drive steam Standard gauge loco made by Lionel known to exist.

In 1920 the pilot wheels on the 6 and 7 changed from cast iron to die cast.

Three different types of headlights were used on the early steamers. They were the slide-on headlight (1908-1911), the pedestal headlight (1912-1918) and the strap headlight (1918-1926).

There were also two different bell sizes. The larger bells were used in 1908 through 1914. A smaller bell was introduced in 1912 and used through 1926.

RATING

The most prized of all the early steamers is the brass and nickel 7 with thin-rimmed drivers, along with its tender with the open three-rivet trucks. More thin-rimmed 7s turn up with the tender with single-rivet trucks, pinpointing production at 1911. About 12 thin-rimmed 7s, with the early tender, are known to exist.

Next in desirability would be the late versions of the 7. Then early versions of the 6 and 5. Later versions of the 5 and 6 are relatively common and worth about half as much as their thin-rimmed counterparts.

Another reason locos with thin-rimmed drivers are so much more in demand is because they look so much better.

1906 Lionel catalog.

ELECTRICS

The early Lionel electrics were copies of the S-1 electrics used by the New York Central railroad and were accurate replicas.

As was the case with the steamers, the first electrics made are the most sought-after by collectors.

Early characteristics included a "square" cab (rather than the later round cab), thin-rim drivers (1910, 1911), script lettering (1910, 1911), "Monitor" roofs and slide-on headlights.

The Monitor roof is what collectors have come to call a separate piece of metal which was soldered to the regular roof of Early period locos.

The 1912, 1913 and 1914 catalogs show round-cab versions of the 33, 34, 38 and 42 with Monitor roofs. No round-cab versions of these locos have ever been found with Monitor roofs. Square-cab versions, with the exception of the four-wheel 53, do have the Monitor roofs.

The early electrics can be confusing. The confusion stems from the fact that a single body style is used with different numbers and occasionally the same number appears on more than one body style. To add to the confusion, sometimes the number of a loco coincided with the year it was introduced and sometimes it didn't. For instance, the 1910 electric was introduced in 1910. But the electrics numbered 1911 and 1912 were also introduced in 1910.

To simplify things, this page has pictures of the various locomotive bodies and the different numbers they carried through the years. The reader should also remember that the locos are discussed in numerical order, not chronological.

Round cab 1910 — 1912 only
33 — 1913-1924
34 — 1912, 1913

Round cab 1911 — 1912 only
38 — 1913-1924
53 — 1920, 1921
50 — 1924 only

1911 Special — 1911, 1912
53 (8 wheel) — 1912-1914
53 (4 wheel) — 1915-1919

1912 — 1910-1911
Square cab 42 — 1912 only
1912 Special (brass) — 1911 only
Square cab 54 (brass) — 1912 only

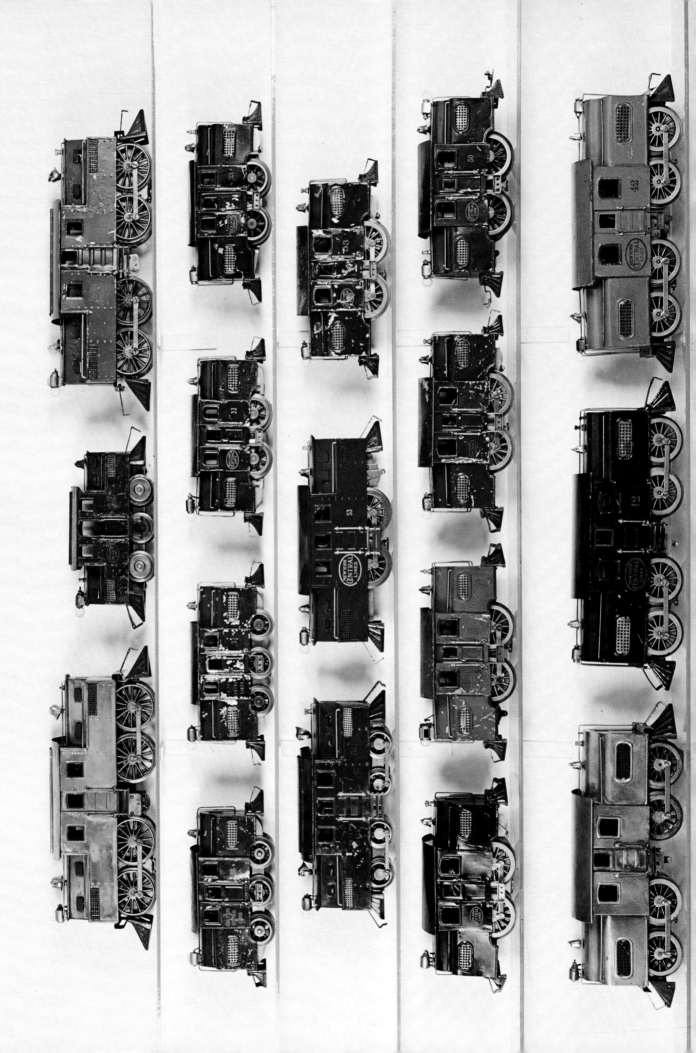

33 ROUND CAB
0-6-0
1913

In 1913 the round-cab 1910 became the 33. It came in dark olive green or black and had either the New York Central oval or Pennsy markings in block lettering. The latter is very hard to find; the black is harder to find than the olive green.

The 0-6-0 33, which ran only one year, had a frame which curved up at the ends and collectors refer to this as the U-frame.

The 0-6-0 33 had six spoked wheels. It came in a set consisting of two short 112 gondolas.

In late 1913 the 33 became an 0-4-0 and this version ran through 1924.

33 ROUND CAB
0-4-0
1913-1924

The four-wheel version of the 33, introduced in 1913, was one of Lionel's most popular engines. It is the version that is familiar to most collectors. It ran through 1924 and came in sets with 100 series freights and 35, 36 series passenger cars.

Colors included dark olive green, black, gray, maroon, red, peacock, dark green and red with cream striping. There was also a very hard-to-find version made specially for Montgomery Ward in 1913. It was painted a beautiful midnight blue and came with two matching 35, 36 series passenger cars. This version had black pilots. Rare regular production models include the red and peacock versions. Olive green and black are the most common.

This four-wheel version of the 33 is known with both the common New York Central markings and the very difficult-to-find C&O markings. The 0-4-0 33s made before 1916 had the U-frame and cast-iron wheels. Those made in 1916 and after had a straight frame and die-cast wheels.

33 — U frame.

33 — straight frame.

A manual reverse was added in 1916 and in 1924, the last year the 33 was available, it came equipped with Lionel's "Super" motor.

A special 33 was made for F.A.O. Schwartz of New York City in 1915. This version was painted black and numbered 60.

34 ROUND CAB
0-6-0 — 1912, 1913
0-4-0 — 1913 ONLY

This was the exact same loco as the 0-6-0 33. The only difference was that it came in a set with two passenger cars (35, 36) while the 33 came with two freight cars.

38 ROUND CAB
0-4-0
1913-1924

This loco was a little larger than the 33 and had an 0-4-0 wheel arrangement with four thick-rim drivers. It ran for 11 years in many different colors. It probably sold more than any other Early-period electric. The 38 used the same body as the round-cab 1911. The 50 and round-cab 53 electrics also used this body, bringing to four the number of locos using the same body: 1911, 38, 53 and 50.

Colors included black, gray, maroon, red, brown, mojave, peacock, red with a cream stripe, and three shades of green. Only one or two peacock versions are known. After that the red, mojave, and the green shades are all hard to find. Black or gray are the most common.

A black 38 also came stamped "62 F.A.O.S." It was for F.A.O. Schwartz in 1915.

42 SQUARE CAB
0-4-4-0
1912 ONLY

There was no difference between a square-cab 1912 and a square-cab 42. They were the same loco.

The 1912 catalog listed outfit 42, which consisted of one 1912 loco plus track. Later in the year they started putting the outfit number on the loco and the number 1912 was no longer used.

Both thin- and thick-rim versions exist and, like the square-cab 1912, the square-cab 42 is known to come in dark green only.

The square-cab 42 is very rare. There are probably less than seven of them.

In 1913 the 42 was given a round cab and this is the version that was available for many years in many different colors.

42 ROUND CAB
0-4-4-0
1913-1923

This loco became the symbol of Lionel. It was pictured on Lionel boxes, featured in the catalogs, and was an example of the best that toy trains could be at the time.

It was big — 15½ inches long, 4 inches wide, and 6 inches high. It was heavy — weighing over 7 pounds. It was powerful — pulling a dozen or more 10 series freight cars. And it was handsome.

The round-cab 42 came in a lot of colors over the years, both regular production and specials. Many odd colors turn up as a result of Lionel's policy of repainting trains that were sent to the factory for repair. This policy undoubtedly created much good will for Lionel but eventually would contribute to the general deterioration of the nervous systems of frustrated collectors who tried to figure out which engines were original and which were factory repaints.

Colors included four shades of green and two of gray, as well as black, maroon, mojave, peacock and red. The red and maroon are the hardest to find, the black and grays the most common. There was also a special version made in black for F.A.O. Schwartz in 1915 and it was stamped "No. 61 FAOS."

The early versions of the 42 had a single motor, three-piece steps, sliding doors and a coupler pocket soldered to the outside end of the loco. In 1918 a single nickel step replaced the original three-piece step and the sliding doors were eliminated. The doors were now fixed. The coupler pocket was now soldered to the inside of the body.

In 1921 the 42 became the first twin-motored loco Lionel ever made and it was harbinger of things to come. In 1923 the twin-motored 402 was introduced and soon after that the big 408E made its debut. This version had a switch for either AC or DC operation.

The 42 was the most significant loco Lionel made in its Early period. It set the trend for the future, and its booming sales helped establish Lionel as the biggest toy train maker in the United States.

50 ROUND CAB
0-4-0
1924 ONLY

The 50 was another loco that was a descendant of the round-cab 1911, which also had been the 38 along the way. The 50 was the last electric introduced in the Early period.

There were actually two versions of the 50, even though it was available for only one year, 1924. The first version used Lionel's standard

motor and came in dark gray, dark green and maroon. Maroon is the rarest. Dark gray is the most common.

The second version, made later in the year, came with Lionel's new Super motor and was available in the same colors as the first version with the exception of maroon. Maroon was replaced by mojave. Mojave is the most sought-after, while dark gray is the most available.

53 SQUARE CAB
0-4-4-0
1912-1914

This loco was available in two wheel arrangements, 0-4-4-0 and 0-4-0. It was the last square-cab electric and used the same body as the 1911 Special. It came in either maroon or brown. This version had eight small wheels, connecting rods, and two bells. New York Central markings in block lettering, script lettering and the oval have turned up.

The 53 was the only square-cab loco continued after 1912.

The maroon and brown versions are about equal in availability.

53 SQUARE CAB
0-4-0
1915-1919

In 1915 the 53 became an 0-4-0, when four thick-rim drivers replaced the eight small wheels. This later version came in maroon, dark olive green and mojave. Mojave is the hardest color to find. Maroon is the most common. The 0-4-0 version of the 53 is known to exist with New York Central markings only and is the only square-cab electric not to have a Monitor roof.

In 1920 the 53 was given a new body, the same one that had been used on the 38.

53 ROUND CAB
0-4-0
1920, 1921

The 53, the only electric that kept the square cab after 1912, lost it in 1920. It was replaced by the same round cab that was being used on the 38. This version came in maroon only with the oval N.Y.C. markings. This is a pretty tough engine to find and is sought-after by collectors.

54 SQUARE CAB
1912 ONLY
0-4-4-0

Since brass locos have no lettering, it is difficult for the novice to tell the difference between a 1912 Special and a 54. They are both brass versions of the square-cab 1912.

The best way to tell the difference is to check the headlight and drivers. If the headlight is the pedestal type and the drivers are thick-rimmed, then it is a 54 made in 1912. If the headlight is the slip-on type and the drivers have thin rims, then it is a 1912 Special. Of the two, the 1912 Special is more highly-prized but both would be welcome additions to any collection. Both are extremely rare.

54 ROUND CAB
0-4-4-0
1913-1924

In 1913 the square-cab brass 54 became the round-cab brass 54. It was the same as the round cab 42 except for the brass. Like the 42, the 54 became a twin-motored loco in 1921 with pretty much the same changes on the doors and steps. The 54s also had two switches, one for AC/DC operations and the other for the manual reverse.

The round cab 54 is only known with thick rims and is the most sought-after of all the round-cab locos but less desired than any of the square-cab locos. Just as split-frame and thin-rims are the most desirable characteristics of Early period steamers, square-cab and thin-rims are the top features of the Early period electrics.

Square cab 1910.

1910 SQUARE CAB — 1910, 1911
1910 ROUND CAB — 1912 ONLY
0-6-0

This was the smallest and cheapest of the new line of electrics Lionel introduced in 1910. It had no reverse. The center wheels were powered and made of cast iron. The two outside pairs of wheels were punched steel. The center wheels generally were set lower than the others, thus making the engine tilt forward or backward.

The 1910 square cab was high and short and really kind of silly-looking. It was rubberstamped "New York, New Haven and Hartford" and was available in its square-cab version in 1910 and 1911. It is known to exist in dark olive green only and was cataloged in a set pulling two short 112 gondolas.

In 1912 the 1910 used the same round-cab body that was used on the 33 the following year. The color remained the same but the loco was now rubber-stamped with the NYC oval.

In 1913 the 1910 designation was dropped and this loco became the 33.

1911
SQUARE CAB — 1910, 1911
ROUND CAB — 1912 ONLY
0-4-0

This loco was a little bigger than the 1910 and not as silly-looking. It came in a set with two 116 ballast cars.

It came with both thick- and thin-rim drivers but is unusual in that the thick-rim version is harder to find. In all other cases when locos have both thin- and thick-rim drivers, the thin-rim version is harder to find.

The 1911 had NYC markings and was painted dark olive green or maroon. Maroon is much harder to find.

In 1912 the 1911 was given a new round-cab body. It was available in dark olive green only. It is known to come with block NYC or with the oval NYC.

The following year, 1913, the 1911 designation was dropped and it became the 38.

1911 SPECIAL SQUARE CAB
0-4-4-0
1911, 1912

This loco had a completely different body from the original 1911. It was a little bigger and designed to go with 180, 181 and 182 series passenger cars and 100 series freights. Most 1911 Specials came with solid wheels but some later versions had spoked wheels. Markings included both NYNH&H in script (early) and NYC in block lettering (later). The trailing truck was weighted to increase traction. Rods connected the small drivers.

The 1911 Special was available in two colors, maroon and brown. Maroon is harder to find.

This was the only square-cab electric that lasted past 1912. The number changed to 53 in 1912, but the square-cab lasted until 1919.

1912 SQUARE CAB
0-4-4-0
1910-1912

This was the biggest of Lionel's Early period electrics. The 1912 was an excellent model of the New York Central's S-type electrics.

It came in this early square cab version with the 1912 number in 1910 through 1912. In the year 1912 the body style remained the same but the number changed to 42. The following year the number remained the same but the body changed to the new round-cab style and the loco ran this way through 1923.

Earliest versions of the 1912 have thin-rim drivers, slide-on headlights and script lettering. Later versions had thick-rim drivers, pedestal headlights and block lettering. It came in dark olive green only and was designed to go with the large 18, 19 190 series passenger cars and 10 series freights.

The 1912 had a single motor, and rods connecting the wheels. Markings included New York Central in block lettering and NYC& HRR in script.

On the early thin-rim 1912, the pilot was angled up, away from the track, to prevent hitting the third rail and shorting. On the thick-rim 1912 the pilot was not angled, but was placed higher on the frame.

The 1912 was the best looking and best proportioned of all the Early period electrics and is to electrics what the 6 is to steamers. The tradition of large electrics, started by the 1912, eventually led to Classic era electrics like the 402 and 408E.

The early thin-rim version with script lettering is the most prized version of the 1912.

1912 SPECIAL SQUARE CAB
0-4-4-0
1911 ONLY

The 1912 Special was the same as the regular 1912 except that it was made of brass. The pilots, grills, vents and wheel spokes were all painted red. It cost almost twice as much as the normal version. It was made for one year only.

The 1912 Special and 7 steamer, both with thin-rim drivers, are the two most sought-after locos that Lionel made in the Early period.

The 1912 Special and the 7 steamer were cataloged with three special cars, the 183, 184 and 185, which were brass versions of the 18, 19 and 190. But the special brass cars were never made, as far as anyone has been able to determine.

RATING

Square-cab versions are always more sought-after than their round-cab counterparts. The most prized of the prized, of course, is the 1912 Special made in 1911 only. Next would be the red or maroon 42 and the square-cab versions of the 1910, 1911 and 1912, followed by the 54.

Here is some more general information about the early electrics.

The inside color and primer color of the square-cab electrics made in 1910 were maroon. The exterior color was green. All 1910 locos used the soldered-on type headlight bracket.

Maroon primer was again used in 1911 but the inside color changed to green. The green exterior color remained the same. Two punched-out "ears" were now used to secure the headlight.

In 1912 the exterior color remained green. Some were still primed in maroon but most used no primer, the green paint being applied directly to the metal. The pedestal headlight made its first appearance in 1912. It was secured by a screw but the "ears" remained although they were not used in securing the headlight.

Square cab 1912 Special.

PASSENGER CARS

The key phrase in this section is "knobbed roof." Passenger cars with knobs on the roof indicate the car was made very early. Knobs also indicate the car is extremely rare.

As with other Early period items, the most prized are the ones that were made first. There is some doubt when the first Lionel passenger car was actually offered for sale. Passenger cars were shown in the catalog as early as 1906 but most collectors feel they weren't actually offered for sale until 1909 or 1910, with the exception of the 29 day coach.

Some of these early cars had funny-looking knobs on the roof that were supposed to simulate ventilators but they were much too big to be anywhere near the correct proportion. Funny looking or not, knobbed-roof passenger cars rank right along with those stratospherically rare, thin-rim steamers and electrics.

Lionel's early passenger cars were constructed of separate pieces of stamped metal that were soldered together. Early cars have open or closed three-rivet trucks, closed clerestories (until 1911), pin-hole steps, long observation decks, early hook couplers, and their numbers are rubber-stamped on the sides.

Later cars have single-rivet trucks, open clerestories, short observation decks, hook couplers and the numbers are stamped on the ends.

A lamp kit appeared in the 1911 catalog. The kit consisted of small lights that clipped to the cars. A wire ran from an electrical post on the loco through the cars and connected the lights to a power source. Lionel illuminated their passenger cars this way until 1923, when roller pick-ups were used and the external wire was no longer needed.

Lionel also sold some miniature models of people made of papier-mache that were designed to sit on the seats inside the passenger cars.

On the early cars with the soldered roof you could get to the inside by unscrewing the bottom. On later cars the bottom was soldered together but the roof was not, instead being secured by a single screw.

29 DAY COACH
1908-1921

The day coach was a passenger car designed for short commuter runs. It had no frills. It had open ends and succeeded the interurban as the main means of transportation for people going in and out of the city.

The day coaches never achieved top billing in Lionel's catalog. The top-of-the-line items were the 18, 19 and 190 series passenger cars. But now collectors prefer the distinctive lines of the day coach. The knobbed versions of the day coach are impossible to collect, however. Only three are known to exist.

The day coach was the very first passenger car Lionel offered for sale and there were three versions of it, all of them numbered 29. The first is called the "trolley-body" day coach. The second is called the "knobbed" day coach. The third version is the one most collectors are familiar with. It is refered to simply as the "29 Day Coach."

The "trolley-body" day coach got its name from the fact that Lionel first advertised a passenger car in their 1906 catalog but didn't actually have one until 1908. That was the year they took the body from a 3 trolley, painted it green, stamped 29 on it and called it their new 29 day coach.

7 with green 19, 18, 190 series high knobs
1912 Special with green 19, 18, 190 series/low knobs
7 with early yellow/orange 19, 18, 190 series
54 with second series orange 19, 18, 190 series
190, 18, 19 with black 42 (partially shown)

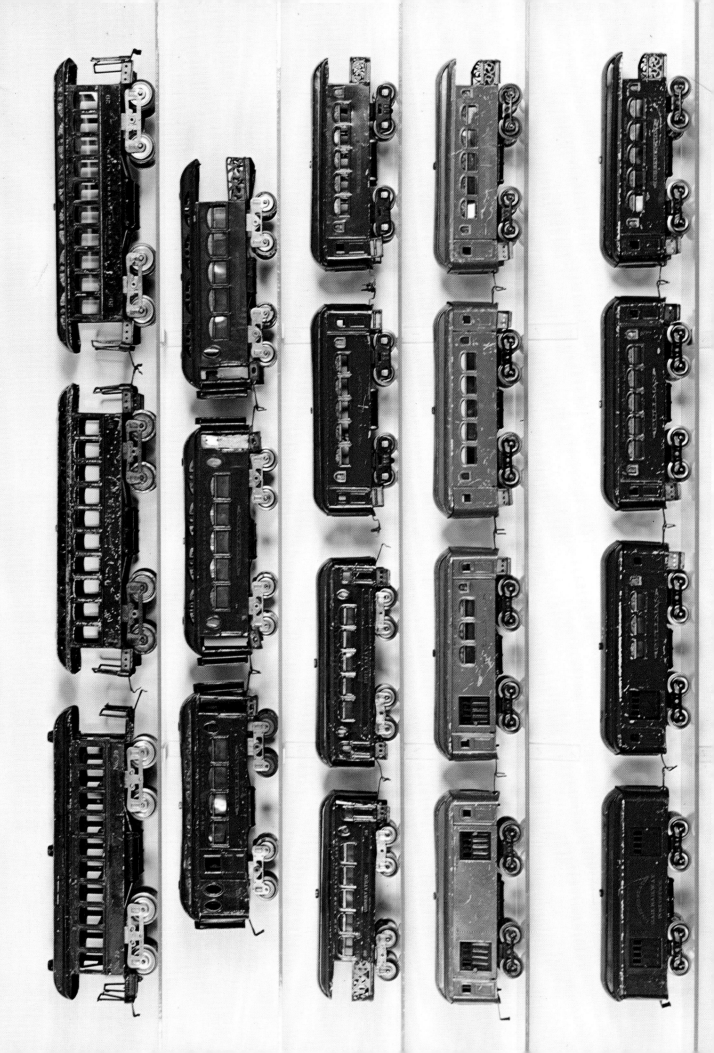

Some trolley-body day coaches have turned up factory-repainted dark green over **orange**, and cream over green and cream. Both were color schemes used on the 3 trolley. What Lionel did was simply take finished 3 trolley bodies and repaint them to make 29 day coaches.

These first version day coaches were stamped "NYC & HRR" between two gold stripes that ran along the side of the car beneath the windows. They had solid or open three-rivet trucks. The trolley body day coaches made in 1908 had closed platform ends identical to the ends on the 1908 version of the trolley.

1909

The trolley body was used again in 1909 but the ends were open, just like the ends on the later versions of the day coach. Open three-rivet trucks were adopted exclusively in 1909 and some day coaches were stamped "Pennsylvania RR, as well as the more common "NYC&HRRR."

Day coaches in 1908 and 1909 were offered for separate sale only.

29 Day coach with open end.

1910

The 29 "knobbed" day coach came out in 1910. It had those odd knobs soldered to the roof, making the out-of-proportion "ventilator." The knobs were about ½-inch high, and the car is now sometimes referred to as the "high-knobbed" day coach (lettered same as 1909 version).

The new body was assembled from individual pieces. The sides were soldered together and the roof was soldered to the sides. The floor was secured by means of four screws.

There were two chains on each platform and the steps were the pin-hole type. The clerestories were closed. The cars were painted maroon and the platforms and steps black. This new body was not too strong, but it was an excellent reproduction of the real day coaches.

The major difference between the day coaches made in 1910 and those made in 1911 was the height of the knobs. The knobs were lowered, measuring only ⅜-inch. Thus the reason why collectors now call the cars the "low-knobbed" day coaches. Another difference was the color. Low-knobbed day coaches were painted green, had open three-rivet trucks, pin-hole steps and "NYC" stamped above the windows.

The preceding description is not beyond dispute, since the sampling of cars it is based upon is limited. Only one low-knobbed day coach is known to exist. It is in the collection of Carey Williams of Glenview, Illinois. For that matter, the sampling of high-knobbed day coaches is not that extensive either. Only two are known. There are eight trolley-body day coaches known to exist.

All of which makes these first versions of the 29 day coach rare in the truest sense of the word.

The last version of the day coach is relatively common and is the one with which most collectors are familiar. It first appeared in 1912 and there were many differences between it and the day coaches that were made before 1912.

The biggest difference was the roof. It was secured by one screw rather than being soldered. The clerestory was now open and celluloid strips were glued to the inside of the roof behind the openings in the clerestory. The air-tanks were smaller than before and they used single-rivet trucks with cut-out bolsters.

The platform was rounded, as in the 1910 and 1911 versions, and the steps were pin-hole-type. The way the number 29 appeared on the sides was changed, too. Before 1912, "No. 29" was used. In 1912 and after, it read simply "29."

This car was painted green with a maroon stripe beneath the windows. The platform and steps were gold. It was made through 1914.

There were some more changes in 1915. Gluing the celluloid to the inside of the windows did not prove satisfactory, so tabs were added to hold the marbleized celluloid more securely. Some were stamped "Pennsylvania RR" but these are hard to find. Most are found with the common "NYC & HRRR" stamping.

29 Day Coach — dark green/low knobs
181 Combination
180 Pullman
35 Pullman — doors at both ends
36 Observation
32 Observation — doors at both ends
32 Baggage — no doors at either end

29 Day Coach — dark green/maroon strip
182 Observation — maroon/second version
35 Pullman — dark green/ribbed
35 Pullman
31 Combination
31 Combination

29 Day Coach — dark green
36 Observation — maroon/500 series trucks
36 Observation — orange
35 Pullman
36 Observation

The platforms were more square than before and had three-hole steps. The trucks were the single rivet, non-cut out bolster type. The ends were painted gold, as were the handrailings and steps. There was also one gold stripe beneath the window. Very late 29 day coaches have the 29 stamped in small lettering, about half the normal size.

The first day coaches came separately. The first cataloged set which included day coaches appeared in 1913. Two 29s were headed by a 51 steam loco. Later day coaches came in sets headed by 42 electrics. No day coaches are known to have been made with illumination.

1910 PULLMAN
1909 ONLY

This was the second passenger car Lionel offered for sale but the first that had a new body designed for use as a passenger car. It is believed to have been made in 1909.

The car was unusual looking because of the placement of the trucks. They were out on the ends of the car, rather than in a little towards the center. Not only did this look strange but it wasn't very efficient. On curves the trucks would bang against steps and derail. Eventually the steps were either removed or they fell off.

The car was totally soldered together. The doors did not open and neither the roof nor the floor was removable. It had three high knobs soldered to the top.

The 1910 came in green only, with open three-rivet trucks. It had "1910" stamped on the sides and, for the first time, "Pullman" appeared in sans-serif lettering.

The 1910 is rare. Only seven are known to exist.

The following year Lionel started production of the large top-of-the-line passenger series. They were given new numbers and the trucks were moved in from the ends, but essentially the new cars used the same body as the 1910.

Lionel also gave several other Early period items the number 1910, including some interurbans, a high-knobbed 18 Pullman, a high-knobbed 19 combination car, and a maroon 1010 interurban.

9 Combine — green/high knobs

8 Pullman — green/low knobs

8 Pullman — yellow/orange

8 Pullman — orange

90 Observation — green

18, 19, 190 SERIES
1906-1927

The 18 pullman and 19 combination cars were first cataloged in 1906 but there is some reason to believe they were not actually made until 1910.

In 1906 there was no photograph shown of the 18 and 19. Instead, the cars were illustrated by an artist's drawing. That same drawing was still being used in 1909, the year that the catalog ran a photograph of their display window set. The 18 and 19 were not pictured in that set, which was normally comprised of the top-of-the-line loco and cars. Collectors feel that had the 18 and 19 been available they definitely would have been included in that set, since they were fancier cars than the two 29 day coaches shown.

By 1910 they definitely *were* available and a 190 observation was added to the series. These early cars had high ½-inch knobs, open three-rivet trucks, air tanks, solid clerestory, pin-hole steps, dish-pan wheels and soldered-on wire handrails. The roofs and sides were soldered together and the floor was secured by four screws. The diaphragms were grooved.

The cars were painted green over a maroon primer and the windows were trimmed in red. They were stamped "NYC."

Hinged doors appeared for the first time and the doors had door handles that were separate metal turnings. The seats did not have the "people pins." There are only two complete sets of these high-knobbed cars known.

The second version appeared in 1911. The knobs were lower — about ⅜-inch high. The 1911 catalog claims removable roofs and pins for the miniature people, but collectors feel this is a description for the 1912 cars — not for the cars made in 1911. Only six sets of the low-knob cars are known.

The 1911 catalog also lists a set of cars that are not known to exist. If they do exist and are discovered they will certainly cause a lot of excitement. The cars in the catalog were identical to the 18, 19, 190 series but they were numbered 183, 184 and 185 and they were suppose to be brass and nickel, to go with 7 or 1912 Special. The idea of a passenger set in solid brass is enough to make an early-period

collector's mind wander during an X-rated movie.

The third version of the series appeared in 1912. The knobs disappeared, people pins were added, and the roof was removable for the first time. Openings were stamped in the clerestory and the celluloid was glued to the inside of the roof behind the openings. These cars are rare.

This series progressed through the years, making the same changes as the 29 day coach. The trucks changed to the single-rivet type and the costly separate door handle was eliminated. The door handle was now simulated and painted gold. On earlier cars the diaphragm grooves were simulated; on this version the diaphragms were smooth.

There were two different kinds of handrails. The handrails toward the middle of the car were stamped out of the body and painted gold. The handrails on the sides of the doors nearest the ends of the cars were separate stampings soldered to the cars. The cars were still painted green and some were stamped "Pennsylvania RR" but most were still stamped "NYC."

The fourth version appeared in 1914. Tabs were added to secure the celluloid behind the clerestory openings and three-hole steps replaced the pin-hole steps.

A new color — light orange — was added in 1916. These new cars were trimmed in cream and were sold in sets with the 7 and 54 locos. Scroll lettering was now used and the numbers appeared on the ends of the car rather than on the sides, as they had before. These light orange cars are rare, too.

The observation deck was shortened in 1918 and the orange color was darkened. Only the window trim was cream. The doors were now maroon. In 1918 the cars were stamped "Lionel Corporation" and the people pins were dropped. By 1920 the orange had become very dark and the window trim changed to maroon, matching the doors.

Lights were added to the series in 1923.

The series was always headed by top locos like the 1912, 42 or 1912 Special electrics. Steamers that came in sets with these cars included the 6 and 7.

The observation deck railings changed through the years. The first cars (1910-1911) had straight slats. The second version (1911-1914) appeared to have heart-shaped perforations. These have turned up on the long decks only. The last type has a serrated or scalloped railing. This type is known on both the long (1915-1918) and short (1918-1927) decks.

Slat railing.   Heart-shaped railing.

Short swirl railing.

The way the doors opened on the 19 combine cars followed a curious pattern. On the first cars with high knobs the doors opened toward the engine. On the low-knobbed cars that appeared next, the doors opened away from the engine. On all other cars made after the knobbed cars, the doors opened toward the engine. Also, the combine car was sometimes lettered "Baggage-Pullman" and sometimes "Baggage-Parlor."

There is also a set of these cars in mojave.

180, 181, 182 SERIES 1911-1921

The earliest cars had pin-hole steps and a solid clerestory. The early color was maroon. The doors were painted dark green. The cars had air tanks and the observation car had the long deck with a heart-patterned railing. Early cars had single-rivet 100 series trucks.

In 1914 some changes were made. The pin-hole step was replaced by the three-hole variety — two small round holes with one large oval hole in the center — and the openings were

stamped in the clerestory. Celluloid strips were visible through the openings. Numbers now appeared on the ends and 180 series trucks were used. The roofs were secured by one large screw in the center.

The short observation platform replaced the long platform. These later cars came with New York Central markings and were painted maroon or brown.

The early versions with the solid clerestory in maroon are the most sought-after cars in the series. Next would come the brown version. The most common are the later cars in maroon.

Two one-of-a-kind paint samples in orange are known to exist. They are the 181 combine and 182 observation. Lionel tried many different colors on their cars to see how they looked. If they decided not to adopt the color for regular production, only the one set would exist. Obviously these are highly valued by collectors and, in this case, only two of the cars have surfaced. Perhaps that is all Lionel needed to make their decision.

35, 36 SERIES 1912-1926
31, 32 SERIES 1921-1925

The bottom-of-the-line passenger cars were initially a two-car series consisting of a 35 pullman and 36 observation. These two cars were introduced in 1912. Two cars were added to the series in 1921 — a 31 combine and 32 full-baggage. The last two added were the first two to go. They were discontinued in 1925. The first two cars lasted a year longer, until 1926. The series was replaced by the Classic-era 332, 337, 338 series.

35 Pullman with ribbed sides.

The early cars can be identified by two embossed ribs that ran the length of the car underneath the windows. The handrails were also embossed and the lavatory windows were oval.

Most of the cars were stamped "New York Central," but some were stamped "Chesapeake & Ohio." At least one car is known, an obser-vation, to be stamped "New York, New Haven & Hartford RR" — spelled out rather than the normal abbreviated way.

These early cars were painted green with four-wheel trucks. The trucks had nickel sides with a single rivet.

A few special cars were made for the mail-order division of Montgomery Ward of Chicago. These were the early ribbed cars and they were painted an unusual and beautiful shade of midnight blue. These cars came in a set headed by a matching blue 33 electric loco. One blue pullman is known to exist without ribs, so it is possible that a complete blue ribless set exists.

Early cars came in two-car sets headed by six-wheel and four-wheel 33 and 34 electrics. Later cars came in four-car sets headed by a 38 electric.

Ribs appeared on the cars made in 1912 and 1913 only. In 1914 the ribs were gone. Early observation cars can also be identified by their long observation decks.

Later cars in the series had no ribs, no handrails, Norman-type lavatory windows and short decks on the observation cars. The clerestory was always closed and the steps were the three-hole version. The later cars used the 100 series truck and came in four-car sets and were painted orange, maroon, brown or the common dark olive green.

The 32 baggage and 31 combine turn up with solid ends, which is the way they should be, or with passenger car doors, the way they should not be. Quality control was not exactly an art form at Lionel in those early years and little things like passenger doors on baggage cars were sometimes overlooked.

The last cars made had combination latch couplers and were illuminated, using the first version of the 500 series trucks with roller pick-ups. The last year the cars were offered, 1926, they came in a two-car maroon set with an 8 electric loco.

The early cars with the ribs are the hardest to find in the series. Of those, the special set in midnight blue made for Montgomery Ward is the most valued. Next would come any car with C&O or New Haven markings, followed by the brown cars, orange cars and maroon cars. The most common — and these are very common — are the late cars in dark green.

FREIGHTS
10 SERIES

The top-of-the-line freight cars in the Early period are referred to as the 10 series. They were introduced in 1906 and as in other categories of the Early period, the versions made first are the most sought-after by collectors.

The cars made between 1906 and 1908 had solid three-rivet trucks, smooth sides and bottom, were primed in yellow, and had the short, straight coupler and two-piece roofs.

The cars made between 1908 and 1911 had open, three-rivet trucks and "Lionel Manufacturing" embossed on the bottom of the cars. The other characteristics remained the same.

The trucks in 1911 changed to the open-type with a single hollow rivet. Simulated wood slats and rivet detail were embossed on the sides of the car. One-piece roofs replaced the two-piece type.

Open truck with large hollow rivet.

Lionel began to paint the cars by dipping them in vats of paint in 1914. Before then they had been sprayed. The cars were no longer primed in yellow and the later, single rivet-type truck was used.

The embossing on the bottom of the cars was discontinued in 1918 and was replaced by rubber stamping. Catalog numbers and "Lionel Corporation" were rubber-stamped in gold on the dark-colored cars and in black on the light colors. Before this, the cars were embossed, "Lionel Mfg. Co."

In 1920 coupler supports were added to eliminate sagging.

The early cars are difficult to find and the late versions are common. There are only

about six complete sets of cars with the solid or open three-rivet trucks known.

The 10 series ran through 1926, when they were replaced by the 200 series freights.

11 Flatcar with handrails.

11 FLATCAR

The 11 flatcar had two sets of four-wheel trucks and a brakewheel. There is not a lot to be said about these cars. Most had no lettering. A very few were made lettered "Pennsylvania." Colors include orange, red, brown, maroon and gray. Orange and gray are very hard to find. Brown and maroon are the most common.

In some of the early catalogs the car was pictured with handrails. Few have turned up with the handrails. One is shown in the photo above.

No load was ever offered with the 11 flatcar.

12 GONDOLA

Early gondolas had the brakewheel soldered to the outside of the car. The top edge was flat, forming a right angle with the side of the car. This resulted in such a sharp edge that Ralph Nader would have demanded a total recall. Later Lionel eliminated the problem by rolling the edge rather than bending it at right angles. They also changed the brakewheel — it was soldered onto the inside of the car.

Colors the gondola came in were red, brown, gray and maroon. Markings included "Lake Shore" and "Rock Island." Some of the cars were trimmed in dark green or pea green. Late gondolas were numbered 65784 and had inspection data on them.

10 SERIES FREIGHTS		
11 Flat — maroon	12 Gondola — red
14 Box — red	15 Tank — maroon
11 Flat — maroon/hand rails	12 Gondola — gray
14 Box — green (Harmony Creamery Car)	15 Tank — maroon
17 Caboose — red/black/awnings	17 Caboose — brown
12 Gondola — red	
13 Cattle — green	
16 Dump — maroon	
13 Cattle — green	
16 Dump — green	

The gondola that is most cherished is painted red or maroon (early colors), has a flat edge and solid, three-rivet trucks, and the brake-wheel is soldered on the outside.

13 CATTLE CAR

The first cattle cars had five slats, a smooth surface and a two-piece roof. In 1911 Lionel began using a one-piece roof and in 1913 they made the openings smaller between the slats by adding another slat. Also around that time embossing detail was added to the cars.

Two-piece roof.   One-piece roof.

The 13 came in many shades of green and had two brakewheels.

14 BOXCAR

The first boxcars featured hand-painted vertical striping on the sides. This was to simulate the wood planking that real boxcars had. These early cars were red and were rubber-stamped "CM&STP." Below this was stamped the number 19050.

Around 1911 Lionel began to emboss the sides to simulate the planking. For awhile they continued to hand paint the vertical stripes, but soon that practice was stopped. About the same time they began marking some of the cars with "NYC&HRR" in addition to the CMSTP markings. Cars with CMSTP had either the number 54087 on the side or the number 98237, while boxcars with the NYC&HRR markings had the number 5906 on the side.

Some of the first embossed cars were painted red. The next color was a yellow-orange. The late cars were painted a darker orange, with embossed sides and without hand-striping. These late cars are quite common.

The most sought after boxcar is the smooth-sided model with hand-painted vertical striping, and either open or solid three-rivet trucks.

HARMONY CREAMERY CAR

In 1921 the Harmony Creamery Company of Harmony, Pennsylvania, purchased a special order of about ten 14 boxcars from Lionel. They were painted dark green, approximately the same color as the Harmony delivery wagons.

Harmony wanted the cars for a special promotion. The company had recently developed the first railroad car that could ship milk. They did this by adding two glass-lined, 2000-gallon, metal tanks to the inside of a boxcar. These insulated tanks kept the milk cold enough for long-distance shipments.

Harmony creamery car, 1920.

To promote their accomplishment, the Harmony Creamery Company ordered the toy boxcars from Lionel, then placed two small evaporated milk cans inside the model, thus simulating the real car. The company also placed their name on the side of the boxcar.

Before Lionel delivered the cars to Harmony, they rubber-stamped the number 14 on the bottom of each car, along with "Lionel Corporation."

There is a postscript to the Harmony story. The company was not totally satisfied with its original milk car, since milk had to be pumped in and out of it at railroad sidings. So Harmony developed a separate milk tank and had it placed on a flatcar.

196 Ives' Harmony creamery car, 1921.

Then in 1922, to promote this car, Harmony went to Ives and purchased about 200 flatcars, then added their little evaporated milk cans to these cars.

Both versions of the Harmony Creamery Car — the Lionel and the Ives — are extremely rare, with Lionel's, of course, being the rarer.

15 TANK CAR

The earliest tank cars had wood domes and wood ends. The paint on these wood parts peeled easily. The cars were painted red or maroon and had a U-shaped wire step. The number 416 with Pennsylvania markings appeared on some early cars. Veteran collectors referred to this maroon color as wine but most collectors now call it maroon. We defer to the old-timers and call the color wine, a word of considerably more romance and poetry than maroon.

U-shaped wire step.   Four-piece soldered step.

One piece, three-hole step.

The tank sits on top of a black girder. Some early catalogs picture the tank sitting on top of a flatcar but it was never made that way.

The next version of the tank car had a three-piece step. In about 1914 metal ends began to replace the wood ends.

All the late tank cars had metal ends and a soldered-on single step with three holes.

The tank car came in red, wine and brown. Wine is the most common. Red is the hardest to find.

The choicest tank car would be painted red, have wood domes and ends, a U-shaped wire step and display the number 416.

16 BALLAST CAR

The ballast car was an operating car. Levers at the ends of the car opened the sides to release the load. Cowen knew even at this early date that cars had to do something more than just ride around the track.

The car came in red, gray, brown, wine and dark green. The late wine color is the most common. The early car in gray is the hardest to find.

The car was rubber-stamped with Pennsylvania markings and the numbers 65784 or 76399 appeared on the sides. The numbers had no significance. They were just added for realism.

The 1906 catalog showed the bin of the ballast car placed on the frame of a flatcar, but this car is not known to have been made. Instead, the bin was mounted on top of a girder, like that on the 15 tank car. The earliest 16 ballast cars had yellow girders, while the later cars had black ones.

17 CABOOSE

The earliest cabooses had awnings over the windows, solid steps leading from the platform, smooth sides, and vertical striping in black. They were painted red with black roofs and stamped "NYC&HRR."

The second version had simulated wood slats with embossing, rather than the painted striping, and the awnings over the main windows were removed. But awnings were added to the cupola windows. The steps remained the same.

17 Caboose with open three-rivet trucks.

The late version had no awnings at all and three-hole steps soldered onto the platform. The cupola tops and windows were rounded rather than square.

Later colors include brown with a black roof and wine with a black roof. The early red version with the awnings is the best one to have.

100 SERIES

The 100 series cars were the bottom-of-the-line freights Lionel offered in the Early period. They were smaller than the 10 series and came in sets with such electrics as the 33, 38, 318 and 8.

There were five cars in the series: the 112 gondola and 116 ballast were introduced in 1910, the 113 cattle, 114 box and 117 caboose in 1912. The series was discontinued in 1926.

112 GONDOLA
1910-1926

The first 112 gondola was introduced in 1910. It was only 7 inches long and is referred to as the short gondola. It was made in only one color combination: dark olive green with red trim. Some were primed in yellow and the yellow is visible on the underside of the floor.

First 100 series truck with pointed bolster.

Second 100 series truck with rounded bolster.

The gondolas were stamped "NYNH&H" or "Lake Shore." The 1910 and 1911 catalogs showed the 112 with Lake Shore lettering and a brakewheel at one end. This version is very rare. More commonly, when the car has a breakwheel, it has the NYNH&H lettering.

The 112 had rivet detail embossed on the side; the top edges of the sides and ends were rounded.

The 1910 catalog listed two sets and they were the first two sets Lionel ever made. One of the sets consisted of two 112s headed by a 1910 electric; the other set had two 116 ballast cars headed by a 1911 electric.

Last 100 series non-flex truck in black. Earlier non-flex trucks were nickel.

Lionel made the 112 bigger in 1912, lengthening it to 9½-inches. The long version came initially in red. Other colors followed, including maroon, brown, light gray, dark gray, and one very rare version of orange. The gondola came with Pennsylvania and Rock Island markings, as well as the Lake Shore and NYNH&H. The ones with Pennsy markings are hard to find. The others are easy to find.

The small version of the 112 is the one that collectors seek. Of the larger version, the early red or orange is the hardest to find. Dark gray is the most common.

113 CATTLE CAR

There is, frankly, little to be said about the 113 cattle car, a car that carried no markings and came in only one color. In 14 years the only thing that changed on the car was its shade of green. It was made from 1912 to 1926, but it is quite hard to pinpoint the manufacturing year of this particular car. The best way, probably, is to look at the trucks. But then again trucks can be changed.

This car, to say the least, has never set off a stampede when discovered at a meet or anywhere else.

114 BOX
1912-1926

The 114 box came stamped "CM&St.P" and came first in red. Later 114s were painted yellow-orange and the last versions were painted a darker shade of orange. The early red is the hardest to find and the later dark orange is very common.

The 114 box used the same rubber stamp markings as the larger 14 box car.

116 BALLAST
1910-1926

The 116 Ballast was in one of the two sets Lionel introduced in 1910, the first sets the company cataloged. One of the sets had two 116s headed by a 1911 loco, while the other set had two 112 gondolas.

The 116 was an early operating car. By turning a handle on the side of the car, doors could be opened and the load released.

Colors included maroon, dark olive green, dark green, brown, gray and dark gray. The dark olive green is the hardest to find, followed by the maroon. The brown and the two shades of gray are the most common colors.

The 116 was stamped with "NYC&HRR." Some came with the number 116 on the side; some came without it.

117 CABOOSE
1912-1926

Both of Lionel's early cabooses had a lot of charm. Hal Carstens, writing about Lionel's Standard gauge, referred to the 117 look as "delightfully railroady." The later series of freights failed to retain this look and these early cabooses are looked upon by collectors with fondness.

"Railroady" 117 caboose.

The early caboose had red sides and a black roof. The next 117s were painted brown with a black roof, and the last versions were painted maroon with a black roof.

The sides of the cupola were sometimes painted black to match the roof or painted to match the sides of the caboose, either red, brown or maroon.

The early coloring is the hardest to find and the later colors are the easiest to find.

RATING

With the exception of the first version of the gondola, all the 100 series cars are common. None, by the late 1970s, was selling for more than $25. Actually, if a collector wanted to start a collection of Lionel's Early period items, he could obtain the late versions of everything except trolleys without difficulty, or without going broke in the process. But if the collector developed more sophisticated taste and became accustomed to thin rims and split frames and brass locos and knobbed roofs, then a serious expenditure of funds would be required.

TROLLEYS

For a number of years trolleys were the hottest selling item in Lionel's line. They were inexpensive — you could buy track, trolley and a transformer for less than $5 — and kids loved them. Trolleys were the main means of city transportation in the early part of the 20th Century. It is not surprising they made popular toys.

Lionel introduced its line of trolleys in 1906, and they were made through 1916. The peak year was 1910, when 13 different powered trolleys and interurbans were featured in the catalog. The popularity of trolleys started to decline about 1913 as people began to buy larger sets and as real trolleys gave way to commuter trains.

Lionel's trolleys were well proportioned and excellent copies of the real trolleys of the time. The young company offered trailers with all its trolleys except the 8 and 9. The early trailers came with the same number rubber stamped on them as their powered counterparts. Most of the later trailers came stamped with their correct catalog number, which was different from the powered unit.

Lionel also made figures of people, which were offered separately, that could be fitted onto the seats of the trolleys. A trolley filled with these passengers was quite colorful.

Most trolleys had "Electric Rapid Transit" written on the side, but some summer trolleys had "Lionel Lines" on the side. The earlier summer trolleys came with serif typeface, the latter with non-serif typeface.

In this section we are concerned mainly with the color combinations of the trolleys and which are the hardest to find — although, of course, they are all hard to find.

When we say one trolley is more common than another, we are not using the word "common" in the same way we use it when referring to, for instance, an 027 postwar steamer. Even the most common trolley is harder to find than a black GG-1, a 746 steamer, or even a Hiawatha. Those are high-priced and desirable pieces, but compared to the most common trolleys — as well as some other early items —

they are not rare. "Rare" in reference to a trolley or other Early period piece means there are only three or four known to exist.

In fact, the authors must confess to a certain imprecision in their use of the word "rare" in their previous books. Had we written this book first, we probably would not have used "rare" as much as we did. "Sought after," "highly prized" or "valuable" — yes. But "rare" — in the sense that these earliest Lionel pieces are rare — no.

By the way, to collect all of Lionel's Standard gauge trolley variations you would have to have about 60. The largest known collection has 33.

A word about the colors that will be discussed in this section. Most Lionel trolleys had two color combinations. The main roof and the letterboard area under the windows were always painted one color, while on the early trolleys the Monitor roof, the window trim, and the stripe under the letterboard were always painted another. They matched the main roof on the late trolleys. When we give the color of any piece, the first color mentioned will be that of the main roof and letterboard, the second color will be that of the Monitor roof, window trim and stripe.

1 with five windows, 1906.

1
4 WHEELS
1906-1914

This little trolley was the smallest and cheapest of all the trolleys Lionel made. It had no reverse or headlight and was made in a number of colors and sizes.

The first version had five windows on each side and non-embossed sides. This early version featured Lionel's "new departure motor" and was the only unit that came with this motor. It was a good thing because it was a lousy motor. Two rubber rollers sat on top of the wheels and transferred the power from the motor to the wheels. This is called friction drive and results in erratic operation. Lionel realized their mistake and discontinued the motor the following year.

"New Departure Motor."

The early version was painted orange and cream and the truck sides were flat with no rivets. In 1906 the 1, with nine feet of track and two dry cell batteries, sold for $4.

In 1907 the five-window 1 came with a trailer painted blue and cream.

1 Trailer, 1908-1909.

The larger second version made its appearance in 1908. The 1 trolley had six windows and was painted blue and cream. Embossed detail was added to the windows. A very rare dark green and cream version was also made in 1908.

Size increased again in 1910. The numbers of windows remained the same but the 1 now used the larger body of the 1908-1909 version of the 2 trolley. So the 1910 version of the 1

was the same as the 2 made in 1908 and 1909, except for the lettering and colors. This last version of the 1 was painted blue and cream.

A very rare version was made for the Maryland Electrical Company of Baltimore, Maryland. It is lettered "Curtis Bay," is painted blue and cream and uses the 1908, 1909 version of the 1 body. Lionel made a number of special trolleys for this Baltimore company and they were all named after trolley lines in the Baltimore area. They are also all very rare.

The 1 always had open platforms and, except for the Curtis Bay, was lettered "Electric Rapid Transit."

The first five-window 1 is the rarest, followed by the Curtis Bay and dark green and cream version.

A 111 trailer was cataloged but is not known to exist.

2 Trailer, 1913-1916.

2, 200 TRAILER
4 WHEELS
1906-1914

This trolley is similar to the 1 but is more deluxe. After 1908 it had both a headlight and reverse. A matching trailer was available and numbered 200, but is commonly found stamped 2, like the powered unit. Both are lettered "Electric Rapid Transit."

The first version was open-ended and came in red and cream and the sides were smooth.

In 1908 Lionel embossed the sides. The 2 came in a red and cream or blue and cream color scheme. The latter is harder to find.

The 2 became a closed-end trolley in 1910. The roof was curved and it is painted red and cream. A matching trailer was also offered with this closed-end version.

8 — dark green/
cream,
reproduction

1 — trailer &
powered —
blue/cream

2 — powered &
trailer — red/
cream

1 — orange/cream,
3 — orange
cream/

1010 — dark green/
low knob,
3300 — green/
maroon, cream/
gold

In 1912 a rare olive green with orange-striped windows was made. The 2 had offset ends (1910-1912) and flush ends (1913-1916). In Tom Sage's collection there is a curious one-of-kind color scheme. It is solid cream with gold lettering.

3 Trolley, orange/cream — 1908.

3, 300 TRAILER
8 WHEELS
1906-1913

The 3 was the first eight-wheel trolley to be offered. The early version had open ends, solid 10-series, three-rivet trucks, non-embossed sides, was painted orange and cream and lettered "Electric Rapid Transit." A trailer was offered, numbered 3 or 300.

3 Trolley, green/cream — 1908, 1909.

Changes were made in 1908. The sides were now embossed and the trucks were the open or closed three-rivet type. The new colors were dark olive and cream or orange and cream. The last color variation is the hardest to find.

More changes in 1910: The 3 came with closed ends and offset platform ends. It was painted dark olive green and cream.

2 Trolley with flat end.   8 Trolley with off-set end.

A very rare version — three are known — was made for the Maryland Electrical Company. It was lettered "Bay Shore."

In 1913 the 3 came with closed vestibules, flush platform ends and was painted dark olive green and cream.

4 Trolley, 1908-1909.

4
8 WHEELS
1906-1913

"Two motors" and "highly prized." These are key words when talking about the 4. It used the same body as the 3 but Lionel added an additional motor. The 4 was cataloged from 1906 through 1912 but no 1906-07 version, which would have had smooth sides and closed three-rivet trucks, has been reported.

The earliest version known is a dark green and cream made in 1908 or 1909. It had embossed sides and closed or open three-rivet trucks. The only other known 4 is a 1913 version with flush ends, also painted dark green and cream.

Lionel's catalog pointed out that the 4 was a very powerful unit and could be used for demonstrations and promotions of one kind or another. Not many 4s were sold as toys.

A matching trailer with the designation of 40 was cataloged but none are known to exist. The 4 sold for about twice as much as the 3.

8
8 WHEELS
1909-1915

Lionel's catalog described the 8 this way: "This model is an exact reproduction of the new 'PAY AS YOU ENTER' cars which are growing so popular throughout the country. Its construction carries out every graceful line found in this type of car, including the large front and rear platforms." The catalog was right. The 8 is a beautiful model of a trolley.

It was the largest trolley Lionel ever made and a fine example of the firm's ability to make quality products.

The earliest 8, introduced in 1909, had nine windows and used the same body as the 3 trolley except that the 8 had long vestibules soldered to each end. This first version was painted orange and cream.

The familiar version of the 8 came out in 1910. It had 11 windows, offset ends and long vestibules. It came in dark olive green and cream and was lettered "PAY AS YOU ENTER."

The early versions exist with open three-rivet trucks only. The later versions come with the more common single-rivet truck.

No trailers were made for the 8. Sometimes the number on the side of the trolley was simply "8" and sometimes "No. 8."

9
8 WHEELS
1909-1912

For trolley collectors this is the ultimate piece. As one collector puts it, "It is super-super-super-super-rare." Fortunately, most collectors interviewed were a bit more articulate than that.

The 9 was the same as the 8, except the 9 had two motors. The first version, introduced in 1909, had nine windows, large closed vestibules and offset platform ends. No trailer was offered. This version was painted orange and cream. Only one or two are known to exist.

In 1910 a larger version of the 9 was made. It used the same body as the 8 in 1910. In fact, it was identical to the 8 except for the number — it was stamped 9 — and the fact that it came with two motors. It was painted dark olive green and cream.

INTERURBANS

In the early part of this century interurbans were the main means of transportation between two close cities or between the downtown and outlying areas.

Perhaps it is the soft memory of a simpler, more placid time that makes trolleys and interurbans so popular today. Or, alas, perhaps it is because they are worth a lot of money. What-

ever, they are gobbled up when they make an appearance at a train meet.

Lionel's interurbans were similiar in appearance to their top-of-the-line 18, 19, and 190 series passenger cars.

10 Interurban with low knobs.

10, 1010 TRAILER
8 WHEELS
1910-1916

The early, most-prized version came with high knobs, solid clerestory, and pinhole steps. It had no doors. It was painted an unusual and beautiful shade of maroon. The knobs were painted black and the trim was gold. This early version is extremely rare.

It came with a single motor and a matching trailer was available, numbered 1010.

Occasionally an interurban that should be stamped number 1010 will turn up stamped 1910. This number turns up on a number of early pieces with no apparent pattern or reason. It is as if there was a mad stamper with a 1910 fetish running amuck in the Lionel factory.

The second version came out in 1911. It had low knobs, pin-hole steps and doors in the vestibule. It was painted green and stamped "Interurban."

Low knob 1010 Interurban.

In 1912 the interurbans came without knobs for the first time. They had open clerestories and were painted green. There was a very rare version made for the Baltimore Electrical Company and it was lettered "WB&A," for the Washington, Baltimore & Annapolis. "Inter-

urban" was stamped in smaller letters above the windows. On this version both the powered and trailer units were stamped with the number 1010. There is no WB&A numbered 10.

In 1914 more changes were made. A pedestal headlight replaced the slide-on type, three-hole steps replaced the pin-hole steps, and a lighting post was added to the rear of the powered unit.

100 Trolley.

100, 1000 TRAILER
4 WHEELS
1910-1916

The first 100s had five windows, closed ends and were painted blue and cream. The trolley featured a headlight but no reverse. It had offset ends and a matching trailer was available, numbered 1000. As usual, more trailers turn up stamped the same number as the powered unit than they do stamped their correct catalog number — 1000. In fact, a trailer stamped 1000 is extremely hard to find, while the 100 powered unit is one of the most common of all the trolleys.

Some changes were made in 1913. The new colors were red and cream and blue and cream. Some of the blue and cream variations were made up special for that Maryland Electric Company and lettered "Linden Ave." The ends changed, too. They were now flush on both the powered unit and the trailer.

The 100 was made a little bigger in 1914 — a window was added to each side. This last version came in the same two colors as the previous version.

SUMMER TROLLEYS

Lionel also made some beautiful summer trolleys. These were accurate reproductions of the open trolleys used in big cities during the first quarter of the 20th century.

101, 1100 TRAILER
4 WHEELS
1910-1913

This was the smallest summer trolley Lionel made. It had a reverse, three reversible benches and was introduced in 1910, the peak year for trolleys. From 1910 on, trolleys lost their popularity to the new, bigger electrics, and were finally phased out completely in 1917.

The 101 had a headlight and came with the 1100 trailer. It was colorful, with a cream Monitor roof, blue main roof, and maroon deck. The sides of the seats were also painted blue and Lionel used lots of gold trim.

Because of the lack of solid siding, however, trolleys were very fragile and are hard to find in good condition.

202, 2200 TRAILER
4 WHEELS
1910-1913

This was a little larger trolley than the 101, having four reversible benches. The 202 also had a headlight, manual reverse and was painted red, cream and black. Its matching trailer was numbered 2200.

3300 Summer trolley.

303, 3300 TRAILER
8 WHEELS
1910-1913

This was an eight-wheel trolley, the largest summer trolley Lionel made. The trailer was numbered 3300.

The Monitor roof was painted cream, the main roof green with maroon trim. This trolley came with reverse and headlight and six reversible seats.

The earliest and most difficult to find 303 came with specially cut-down three-rivet trucks. The trucks had to be cut down so the trolley could negotiate Standard gauge curves.

404, 4400 TRAILER
8 WHEELS
1910-1912

Another twin-motored trolley was cataloged but is not known to have been made. The trolley depicted in the Lionel catalog uses the same body as the 303 trolley but was numbered 404. A 4400 trailer was also cataloged but is not known.

1011, 1012 TRAILER
8 WHEELS
1910-1912

There was one twin-motored interurban cataloged. It was stamped 1011 and came with a trailer unit stamped 1012. There is no evidence that either was ever made. At least none have turned up.

RATING

As might be expected with something as scarce as trolleys, most collectors don't know anything about them.

On those remarkable occasions when trolleys are found, they are not usually in good condition. Flaking paint is the major problem, particularly on the Monitor roof. Sometimes trolleys have turned up in excellent condition except for one thing — the Monitor roof has no paint left on it. The paint Lionel used in the early years was sensitive and would not adhere to a surface that was not properly cleaned.

Some misnumbered trolleys have also turned up. Those reported are a 100 and 202, both stamped "No. 1." Trolleys also appear with factory repaint jobs like a 3 stamped "Bay Shore" painted over a 300 trailer and a 1 Curtis Bay repainted over a 1908-1909 number 1.

The collector must remember that Lionel was in the business of moving inventory and if repainting helped get rid of some old stock lying about the factory, then new paint and stampings were applied and out went the item. There was no thought given to the problems this would cause collectors sixty years later. No one even knew there would be such a thing as a collector. Joshua Cowen was concerned about finding customers, not collectors.

The most desirable and hardest-to-find trolley is the 9 with double motors, in either the nine-window version or the eleven-window version.

Ranking right behind the 9 would be a nine-window 8, any 4, the first version of the 1 with five windows, any maroon, high-knobbed interurban, the 303 summer trolley and the 3300 trailer.

Also in this list would be all the special trolleys made for the Maryland Electrical Company. Those that have turned up include the 1 Curtis Bay, 3 Bay Shore, 100 Linden Ave. and the 1010 W.B.&A. Others that were also cataloged in 1911 but that have not yet shown up include the 2 Edmondson Ave., 8 Gilmore Ave., 101 Wilkins Ave., 303 Madison Ave. and 202 Preston Ave.

The trolleys that turn up the most include the later 2s, the large version of the 8, 100s and late green interurbans.

Lionel 402 with prototype in the background. Three of these old NYC S-type electrics are at the Croton-Harmon yards, formerly the steam maintenance facilities on the New York Central's four-track water level route. Here steam engines were swapped for electrics, and vice-versa, as steam couldn't enter city limits. Croton-Harmon is about an hour north of New York.

CLASSIC PERIOD

The "Classic period" is the name most collectors have given to the Standard-gauge trains Lionel made from 1923 until 1942. There is no particular reason for the name; it is just a way of delineating between the early trains and the later. Not all collectors even use the term "Classic period." Two who do are Hal Carstens of Carstens Publications and Howard Godel, author of the fine *Antique Toy Trains.* Godel says the later trains remind him of classic automobiles of the 1930s.

In any case, we wanted to call these later trains *something* and went along with "Classic," perhaps because Howard Godel once complimented us on our books. We immediately decided he was a man of excellent taste and if he chose to call the later trains "Classic," that was good enough for us.

What distinguishes the later trains from the earlier ones, to perhaps over-simplify, is that the later ones had more authentic detailing, more brass and nickel trim, and came in brighter colors.

The locomotive that started the Classic period was the 402 electric, which came out in 1923.

But it was not until 1927 that Lionel had used up their old inventory of early items, and the catalog was filled with nothing but the newer models. Therefore, between the introduction of the 402 in 1923 and the issuance of the 1927 catalog, there was a certain overlap of Early period and Classic period pieces.

Electrics had the Classic period to themselves for several years. It was not until 1929 that the first of the new steamers made its appearance with the introduction of the 390. The new electrics were modeled after the New York Central's S-class, the Milwaukee Road bi-polars and the Pennsylvania's BBB-style electrics.

Most of the early Classic locos — the ones made during the overlap years 1923 to 1927 — have combination latch couplers, strap nickel headlights and brass trim. Later locos, 1927 and after, have latch couplers, cast headlights and brass trim. Bodies and frames were made of stamped metal on all of the electrics.

Almost all electrics were available with or without the automatic reverse unit, which was introduced in 1926. The letter "E" was used to designate a loco with the automatic (electric) reverse.

ELECTRICS

8/8E
0-4-0
1925-1932

This was the smallest and cheapest electric Lionel made. It is also the most common. It headed sets that included 500 series freights or 337, 338 passenger cars. When it first appeared in the 1925 catalog, it was shown with one headlight. All known versions have two headlights, one pantograph and a whistle.

The 8E was the only electric Lionel made that had the reverse lever coming out the end rather than the side.

It was made in an assortment of colors both cataloged and uncataloged. Cataloged colors included maroon, olive green, mojave and red. Uncataloged colors were dark olive green, maroon with a cream stripe and cream window trim, peacock, pea green and dark green.

All the uncataloged colors are more sought-after than the cataloged colors. The uncataloged colors are all prized, with the olive green and peacock being the two most difficult to find.

All the cataloged colors are common, with the exception of mojave. Maroon and olive green are the most common.

The red version exists with a cream stripe at the bottom of the cab and cream window trim and with no stripe and brass window trim. The all-red without the stripe is more valuable.

Most models have brass inserts behind the ventilators. The peacock version had orange inserts. The pea green version had yellow inserts.

There is an unusual variation having to do with the vents on the side of the loco. Most have six openings, but a very few were made with only three openings.

9/9E/9U
0-4-0, 2-4-2
1928-1936

This was one of Lionel's most interesting electrics. It came three ways: with manual reverse (9), with electric reverse (9E), and in kit form (9U). The "U" designation in Lionel language meant "You build it."

This locomotive closely resembled the 8, but was a little longer. Like the 8, it had a single motor. But it cost more than the 10 — or the 8 for that matter — and never sold well. It didn't have anything to offer that the 8 didn't. Because it did not sell well, it is now among the hardest to find of all classical Standard-gauge locos.

The hardest color to find is the hand-reverse dark green 9. This version has neither pony wheels nor trailing wheels. These 9s have the same reversing unit as the 9U, but the number plate reads 9.

The next hardest color to find would be the orange 9E or 9U. The kit form 9U is the rarer of the two. Next would be the two-tone green 9E that headed the three-car Stephen Girard set. This 9E does have both pony and trailing wheels but lacks the Monitor roof like the earlier orange and dark green versions. The most common color is the gray 9E. This version also has the pony and trailing trucks.

The dark green 9 and the orange 9's have a raised section on the roof. The Stephen Girard 9E and the gray 9E have flat roofs.

9E with flat roof.

Some orange 9Es and dark green 9s came with laminated, weighted frames. The additional weight was required to pull the 428, 429, 430 series passenger cars.

10/10E
0-4-0
1925-1930

This was the second smallest electric Lionel made. It came in a number of colors, both cataloged and uncataloged. The uncataloged red 10E, with or without the cream stripe, is the most sought-after by collectors. Other uncataloged colors included tan, olive, peacock with an orange stripe and dark green frame, and State brown with a dark green frame and cream stripe. The 10E in peacock with the dark green frame came with a "Bild-A-Loco" motor.

Cataloged colors included peacock, mojave, and gray. The most common colors are peacock and mojave. All the uncataloged colors are harder to find than the cataloged, with the brown and red first and second in scarcity.

318/318E
0-4-0
1924-1935

A medium-priced loco, it headed sets with 500 series freights and the 339, 341 series and 309, 310, 312 series passenger cars.

Some of the colors it came in are quite scarce. By far the hardest to find is the all-black 318E that headed the coal train. This set included three 516 rubber-stamped hoppers and the red and black 517 caboose. Next in scarcity would be the 318 or 318E in State brown. This loco headed three 309 series cars and is referred to as the Baby State Set. After the State brown would be mojave.

The most common colors are gray and pea green.

The late 318E in brown came with the Lionel "Bild-A-Loco" motor.

380/380E
0-4-0
1923-1929

This was another medium-sized and priced engine. It usually came in sets with 200 series freights and 319, 320, 322 series passenger cars.

Some late 380Es came in sets with the larger 428, 429, 430 series passenger cars. To give the added traction required to pull these heavier cars, weights were added to each end of the loco's frame.

The brass plates came three different ways. One had both black lettering and a black border; a second had black lettering and a red border, and the third had both the border and lettering red. The third is the most common version and the first is the most difficult to find.

The hardest color to find is mojave, the easiest is the maroon. It also came in dark green.

381 (manual reverse).

381/381E/381U
4-4-4
1928-1936

This was the largest and flashiest electric Lionel made but it was not the most powerful nor the most expensive. The twin-motored 408E surpassed it in both categories. Nevertheless it is the most highly prized and valuable Lionel electric of the Classic era.

The 381E in the color photograph on page 52 is a reproduction, made by Williams Reproductions of Baltimore, Maryland. An original 381 is shown above and on page 64 heading a set of State cars.

There is a continuing argument among collectors over the use of reproductions. Generally, reproductions have not had much effect on the price of originals. But some collectors feel they lower the price of originals by reducing the demand. Others feel that in some cases reproductions have actually increased the value of the original by creating new interest in it.

The 381E was a good model of the electric used by the Milwaukee Road over the mountainous stretch between Othello and Tacoma, Washington. In our book on Lionel postwar we show a photo of a custom-made O gauge bi-polar made from a GG-1 frame and trucks.

The bi-polar made by Lionel came three different ways. The most common by far is the 381E. This version had the automatic reverse and "381E" appeared in red on the brass number plates on both sides of the loco.

Some 381s with a manual reverse have turned up. These are hard to find. The manual reverse versions had a plate on one side of the engine and the manual reverse switch on the other. The plate said simply "381", etched in black against the brass background.

The 381 comes in dark State green. The 381E comes in State green. Both have apple green sub-frames.

Early 381Es had a pea green background behind the brass vents on the side. Later 381Es had a brass plate behind the brass vents.

There was also a kit model, numbered in the catalog 381U, but no 381U plates have surfaced. Whenever a kit has been found, not yet assembled, the number on the plate has always been 381, the same plate that came with the manual reverse versions.

If a kit version with a 381U plate ever does show up it will be the most valued version of the 381. But so far the most valued is the 381 with the manual reverse.

402/402E
0-4-4-0
1923-1929

This twin-motored workhorse had great pulling power, far more than the larger 381E, which only had one motor. In looks, it was similar to the 408, but did not have as much trim. One of its distinguishing features was that only one headlight would shine at a time, the one facing the direction in which the loco was traveling.

It headed the top-of-the-line set, which consisted of three 418, 419, 490 series cars, until 1927 when the 408E was introduced.

The E designation, as it was on other electrics, was either etched in the brass number-plate, or rubber-stamped on the door. Some-

times Lionel used old inventories of plates without Es on their locos that had the reversing unit. When this was done, the letter E would be stamped in black on the door. Locos with the E stamped on the door are much harder to find than locos with the E after the number on the brass plate.

The 402s, whether the E version or not, had a hole punched in one end of the frame. This was for a car-lighting bracket, used when cars did not have illumination. A separate lighting kit was sold that included lights and wire. The wire would then be strung from car-to-car and hooked up to the bracket on the engine frame.

After 1923, when the large series passenger cars received their own illumination, the car-lighting bracket was no longer used, but the hole was still punched in the frame of the engine.

Most collectors consider only two versions of the engine to be collectable: the early version with the strap headlight, and the later version with the cast headlight. Only one color was ever cataloged — mojave. There were a number of color samples tested by Lionel, and these one-of-a kind sample cars are the most valued of all the 402s. One sample color was mustard. A mojave-colored engine that was factory repainted over a dark green showed up once, so there is a possibility that some dark green models were made.

The 402/402E is a common engine in mojave. Naturally, it is not common in any of the one-of-a-kind color sample models.

As a postscript to the 402s, we must mention Fred Ziegler, a collector from York, Pennsylvania. Ziegler has 22 402s and 402Es on a layout in his basement. These 22 big engines pull a single caboose, and Fred calls this "The Thundering Herd". He claims each loco is different in some way from the other, whether by various combinations of trim, color shades, paint texture or any other minor difference. It is a wonderful thing to see, Ziegler's Thundering Herd, but a discussion of its minute variations will have to be put off for some future work.

Two-tone brown 408E.

408E
(1927-1936)

This was the same engine as the 402, but with large operating pantographs and additional handrails on the roof. It also had four inset lights that the 402 did not have, two at each end. It does not exist without an automatic reverse.

It was introduced in 1927 and was the top-of-the-line loco for one year. Then, in 1928, the 381 was introduced and it became the top-of-the-line leader. But it was discovered that the 381 was unable to pull the four-car State Set and the more powerful 408E, which had been heading smaller sets, was chosen to pull the top-of-the-line State Set.

Most of the 408Es came with the Lionel Super motor, but some are available with the Bild-a-Loco motor.

The normal color of the 408E that headed the State Set was either all-tan or tan with a dark brown roof. Some turn up painted dark green. This came about because sometimes the factory repainted them dark green. Occasionally customers, unhappy with the weak performance of the 381, would send it back to the factory.

Dark-green 408E.

Lionel would then replace it with the 408E, first repainting it the same dark green color as the 381. Actually, there were two shades of dark green that were painted over the 408E's: the darker shade that the roof of the State cars were painted, and the lighter shade that the sides of the car were painted. The lighter dark green is harder to find.

It did not happen often that a customer returned a 381 for a 408E. Hence, the factory repaints are highly prized by collectors.

Besides the tan, the regular production colors of the 408E included mojave and apple green. Of the production colors, the most valued is the tan with the dark roof. Then comes the all-tan and then the mojave. Apple green is the most common.

Pink 408E.

The 408Es were also made in a number of special and uncataloged colors, including cream, pink, and gray. All of these, of course, are extremely rare.

A crackle-dark green 408E emerged some years back, and a picture of it is shown, but its legitimacy has been seriously questioned.

408E dark green crackle finish.

RATING

Of the Classic period electrics, the hardest to find is the 381 with the hand reverse. Next in order, are: (2) either version of the dark green 408Es; (3) the 408E in brown, either version; (4) the 9 in dark green; (5) the 381E.

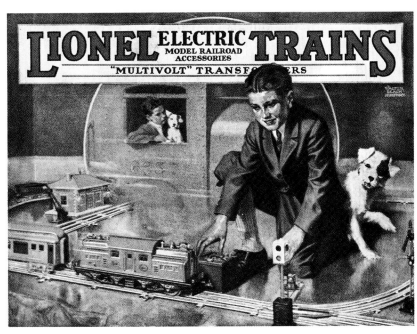

1925 Lionel catalog.

STEAMERS

Lionel held off bringing out their new line of steamers until 1929, even though the new electrics debuted in 1923. The electrics were easier to manufacture because they had less detail and fewer moving parts than the steamers.

During the twenties Lionel's competition was making heavy die-cast and cast iron steam locos and they were doing well with them. Lionel decided to make their steamers differently. They made their boilers of stamped metal and the frames and steam chests of pot metal. Brass and copper trim were added along with some red paint to brighten things a bit. The result was a flashy, well-built toy loco that compared well with the competition.

Lionel used no actual prototype. They simply made a toy steam engine and any similarity to the real thing was purely coincidental.

As with the electric, there were certain characteristics of the steamers that indicated when a particular model was built. Early classical steamers had brass and copper trim, while the later versions had all nickel trim.

In most cases the later, nickel versions are the most desirable.

384, 384T — black
390E, 390T — black
385E, 384T gunmetal
1835E, 1835T (Ives)
392E, 392T

384/384E
2-4-0
1930-1932

This was the smallest, cheapest, most common, and least interesting of all the Lionel Standard gauge steamers.

The 384, without the automatic reverse, came with or without a green stripe and either brass window trim or green window trim.

All the 384Es came with a green stripe and either brass or green window trim.

The 384/384E came with 500 series freights (three-car sets) and 338 or 309 series passenger cars.

The 384/384E came with a 384T tender and, depending on what cars it pulled, had either nickel or brass journals.

385E
2-4-2
1933-1939

The 385E came equipped with the "Chugger", Lionel's first attempt to simulate the sound of a real steam engine.

The early versions were painted gun metal gray, had copper and brass trim and red driving wheels. The red pony wheels came either solid or spoked.

Later versions of the engine were painted a darker shade of gray, had nickel trim, painted boiler bands and black driving wheels. The pony wheels, also painted black now, came in the spoked variety only.

The 385E pulled the Ives transition passenger cars and 500 series freights.

The 385E came with the 384T tender in 1933 and 1934 and the ex-Ives die-cast 385T tender in 1935 through 1939. This tender is very difficult to find in good condition. Usually it is found in some state of decay because impurities were mixed in with the lead and zinc when the bodies were cast.

The early 385E with copper trim is the most sought-after by collectors.

390/390E
2-4-2
1929-1931, 1933

The 390/390E was Lionel's start in the toy steamer derby and it was a good start. It came in a number of attractive colors and combinations of brass and copper trim. Contrasting striping on the running boards and tender added a finishing touch of elegance to this handsome loco.

The 390/390E does not exist with nickel trim and usually came in sets comprised of 500 series freights and 309, 310, 312 series passenger cars. We say usually because in 1930 the 390E headed the first Blue Comet set. The next year the 400E was introduced and of course it replaced the 390E as the top-of-the-line steamer and also replaced it at the head of the Blue Comet set. This same year, 1930, the 390E was cataloged in a set with 200 series freights. This was the last time these large freights were cataloged with any steamer other than the 400E.

To accommodate the higher coupler on the 200 series cars the 390E came with a special tender. It had 200 series trucks and was designated 390X. The normal tender that came with the 390 was designated 390T and had 500 series trucks.

The color most difficult to find is the dark green 390E with the frame painted either a matching dark green or a contrasting light green. This loco has an orange stripe on the running board and brass trim.

The second most sought-after 390E is the blue version that headed the Blue Comet set in 1930 only. This loco and its tender had a cream stripe. The sandomes and smokestack were copper. The rest of the trim was brass.

There was also a black 390E with a red stripe and a black 390E with an orange stripe.

The 390 with the hand reverse, made in 1929 only, is difficult to find but mostly ignored by collectors, who prefer the more exotic Blue Comet and dark green versions.

392E
4-4-2
1932-1939

Next to the 400E, the 392E was the largest Standard gauge locomotive Lionel made. The earliest version was painted black with brass and copper trim. This early 392E came with a 384T Tender. The tender came with or without a green stripe and some are known to exist with a black crackle finish.

The 392E also came with a large 12-wheel tender designated 392T. The first 392Es that came with this tender were black with brass and copper trim. Later 392Es that came with this large tender were painted either black with nickel trim or gray with nickel trim.

The 392E also featured a red light under the cab to simulate the glow from the firebox on a real train and a chugger unit.

The most common is the early version with the small 384T tender. The hardest to find is the 392E with the black 12-wheel tender. Next in desirability would be the gray version with the 12-wheel tender.

400E
4-4-4
1931-1939

The 400E was the Big Daddy of Lionel's Standard gauge steamer fleet. Introduced in 1931, the 400E immediately moved to the front of the top-of-the line sets.

The 1931 catalog ballyhooed the 400E's arrival with a cover photograph of Bob Butterfield, the engineer of the New York Central's 20th Century Limited. Butterfield was shown holding a 400E while standing in front of a NYC Hudson. Butterfield's two grandsons were looking up at the veteran engineer while he was supposed to be telling them, "Just like mine," referring to the supposed similarity between the Lionel model and the real Hudson.

The only thing was, the real Hudson had a 4-6-4 wheel configuration, while the 400E, of course, was a 4-4-4 and only vaguely resembled the Hudson. But it made a good selling feature and Joshua Lionel Cowen was not one to let the absence of one driving axle stand in the way of a good advertising gimmick.

Years later, by the way, after Butterfield retired, he said, "Well, it was not *quite* 'Just like mine.' "

The 400E was the only loco to pull the large 200 series freights, except for the 390, which headed them in 1929 and 1930. The tender which came with the 400E was the 12-wheel Vanderbilt type, the 400T. The early 400T tenders had ladders without a support span, while the later 400Ts had a span added.

400T without extra ladder support.   400T with extra ladder support.

The early tenders came with black lettering on brass nameplates. The later gray tenders came with the nameplates that were nickel with a red background and nickel lettering.

400E with "clip-on" hand rail clips.

400E with turned-brass handrail clips.

Early 400Es had clip-on hand rail stanchions. Later 400Es had turned hand rail stanchions.

The 400E came in sets with the Blue Comet, State cars, and the 418, 419, 490 series passenger cars.

The earliest version of the 400E, the one that came out in 1931, was black with brass and copper trim, and either cast or brass journals on the tender. This is the most common of the 400Es, of which there later were at least 30 variations.

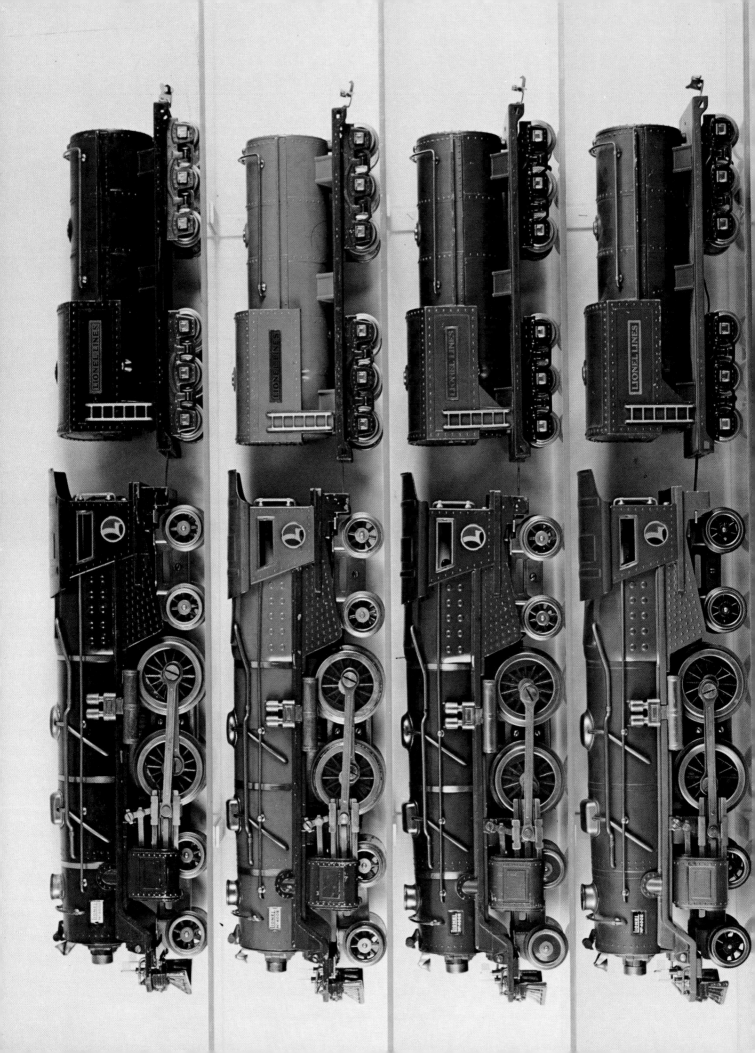

Among the many variations were: gun metal with copper and brass trim and brass journals on the tender; gun metal with copper and brass trim and painted boiler bands; gray with nickel trim; black crackle paint, with brass trim; and black with nickel trim.

The early Blue Comet-400Es came in a darker blue than the later Blue Comets. This led to additional variations. The dark blue early versions had brass and copper trim, while the lighter blue later versions had nickel trim.

The hardest of the 400Es to find is the black model with nickel trim. There was such a limited production run of these that there were probably no more than a few dozen of them made. Only slightly more numerous is the black crackle model with brass trim. An original black-crackle 400E is shown on page 92.

The next hardest to find is the later, light blue Blue Comet with nickel trim.

In addition to these production models, there are a couple of other variations that should be mentioned. There was a 400E made early that was a shade of blue that was a bit more purplish than the early Blue Comet dark blue. This had brass and copper trim, but only two of them are known to exist, one with a red stripe and one without.

There are also a couple of one-of-a-kind 400Es. One is green, the same shade as the State cars. The other is black with a red stripe along the running board.

1835E
2-4-2
1934-1939

The 1835E used the same body as the 385E. The main difference was the 1835E did not come with a chugger. The 1835E is known in black only with black boiler bands, wheels and nickel trim.

Except for the first year — when it came with a 384T tender — the 1835E always came with an 1835T tender with the Ives cast body. This Ives tender — painted black — usually is found in good condition unlike the Ives tender — painted gray — that came with the 385E, which is usually found in some advanced stage of decay.

The most desirable 1835E set would be the one comprised of the two-tone blue 309, 310, 311 series passenger cars.

The 1835E is one of the more common Standard gauge locos and does not cause much excitement.

RATING

Almost all the versions of the 400E are more sought after than any other Classic period steamer. Possibly the black 392E with the 12-wheel black tender is more valuable than the most common version of the 400E. Next would come the green 390E, then the blue 390E. The 384 is the most common.

400E, 400T — black/brass & copper trim
400E, 400T — medium blue/dark blue/brass & copper trim
400E, 400T — gun-metal gray/brass & copper trim
400E, 400T — gray — nickel trim/painted boiler bans

1835E.

PASSENGER CARS

The big-name passenger cars from the Classic period are the premier items of Lionel Standard gauge, both from the standpoint of the money they cost and the prestige connected with having them in a collection. The sets in the photograph on the opposite page, for example, were worth $25,000 on the 1977 collector's market, and there was no indication that the price would not continue to rise.

But there is an interesting irony connected with the demand for, and the adulation of, the large passenger cars. They are not rare. In fact, the green State cars are relatively easy to find. But so many collectors consider them rare, or consider a Standard-gauge collection *déclassé* without them, that they command huge prices. They are among the most valued toy trains in the world.

In the late 1920s and early 1930s, as Lionel was emerging as the dominant company in the toy train field, these top-of-the-line passenger cars symbolized that domination. Some of the cars are among the best and most detailed mass produced toy trains ever built.

This section will cover all the large, more exotic sets, as well as the ordinary and lower priced series that were available between 1923 and 1942.

Passenger cars follow the same basic patterns as freight cars. Early cars were trimmed in brass, transition cars used a combination of brass and nickel trim, and late cars had all-nickel trim. In most cases the late versions are the most valued.

Journals were cast or nickel early, were brass later, and were nickel very late. Window material was mostly clear plastic but on some of the very late cars it was frosted.

The cars that were rubber-stamped were mostly stamped "Lionel Lines." Less common stampings would be "New York Central Lines," and the least common would be "Illinois Central."

412, 413, 414, 416 SERIES "STATE CARS" 1929-1935

The Lionel State cars were the most elaborate toy train passenger cars ever mass-produced in the United States. One would have to look to European manufacturers to find comparable cars.

The cars featured hinged roofs, illumination, revolving armchairs and had two lavatory compartments on all cars but the observation, which had one. Even the toilet seats were hinged. The cars were 21 inches long, 7 inches high, and weighed almost 6 pounds. They were built to take a pounding, too. The cars were trimmed in brass and had six-wheel trucks. There was a great deal of handwork required in assembling the cars and because of this, restoration experts normally charge more than $100 to restore a State car. Each seat has to be removed and replaced individually.

State car truck with cast journals.

None of the top-of-the-line cars of Lionel's competition — Ives, American Flyer, or Dorfan — came close to matching State cars in detail.

The first State set appeared in 1929. It was not called a State set. The catalog called the set the "Transcontinental Limited." Collectors

State Set — green/dark green/light green window trim — 381E, 412, 413, 414, 416
State Set — brown/dark brown — 408E (dark brown roof), 412, 413, 414, 416
State Set — black 400E, 400T — green/dark green/cream window trim — 412, 413, 416
State Set — brown/dark brown — 408E (tan roof), 412, 413, 416
State Set — green/dark green/light green window trim — 381, 412, 413 brown/dark brown — 416

came to refer to the set as the State set because each of the cars is named after a state. The three Pullmans were the 412 California, 413 Colorado and 414 Illinois. The observation was the 416 New York. The cars were painted green with darker green roofs and lighter apple green window trim.

That first year, 1929, the four-car State set was headed by the 381E electric. This was the only four-car State set headed by the 381E. The 381E was big all right but it wasn't strong enough to adequately pull 24 pounds of State cars. The next year, Lionel headed the four-car State set with the twin-motored 408E and had the 381E pull a three-car State set. The Illinois pullman was eliminated from the four-car set. That is why Illinois is the rarest of all the green State cars. It was available in the 1929 set only. All State cars, including the Illinois, were available for separate sale through 1935. The three-car State set headed by a 381E was cataloged through 1934 and called the *Olympian.*

The green State cars also came in a three-car set headed by the 400E steamer. This set was first cataloged in 1931 and was available through 1933.

The green State cars changed somewhat through the years, developing into four main versions.

The first version, with the dark green roofs and apple green window trim, had cast journals and the ventilators on the roof were painted the same green as the sides of the car.

About 1931 or 1932, the journals changed to brass.

The next change had to do with the ventilators. They were now painted the same dark green as the roof rather than the lighter green of the sides.

The last version — and the version that is the hardest to find — made one big change. The windows were trimmed in cream rather than apple green.

Brown State cars were also available. The brown State set, headed by a brown 408E, is the most valuable and sought-after single set Lionel ever made.

The first brown State set was cataloged in 1930, after it was decided a twin-motored loco was needed to pull the four State cars. Brown State sets were always four-car sets and they were cataloged through 1933. They were painted tan with dark brown roofs.

On the earliest versions the roof vents were painted tan and the cars came with cast journals. The next version had brass journals. The late brown cars eliminated the extra step of giving the roof vents their own color. The vents on the last cars were painted the same dark brown as the roof. All the brown State cars had cream window trim.

The 408E that pulled the earlier sets was tan with a dark brown roof. Later 408Es were painted solid tan. The two-tone 408E is much harder to find.

Brown cars are all hard to find. No one version is rarer than the others. The key to acquiring any set of State cars is to make sure that they are a matching set.

The most valued State set would be any four matching brown cars with a two-tone 408E. An original set in like-new condition sold at auction for $7,000 in the fall of 1976.

The hardest to find State cars, though not the most valuable, are the green with the cream window trim. Most collectors do not realize how rare these cars are. Fewer of the green cars with cream trim turn up than any other version of the State cars, including the brown.

The early green State cars with the apple green window trim are quite plentiful and are readily available to anyone who wants to pay the price.

420, 421, 422 SERIES "BLUE COMET" 1930-1938

This is the only big passenger set that collectors call by the same name that Lionel did in its catalog. By 1930 other toy train companies had begun to name sets after well-known trains of the day and Lionel decided to jump aboard the trend with their version of the Blue Comet, a fancy Jersey Central special that made a weekend-oriented run from Jersey City to Atlantic City, by way of New York City.

The prototype was painted a dark blue with a black roof and a cream stripe across the windows. Boucher's Blue Comet was painted very similar to the prototype, but Lionel, after painting a few sets dark blue with a black roof, decided to go with a more attractive color scheme — dark blue roof, medium blue sides and a cream window trim. Lionel was in the business of selling toys, not of being accurate. The result was one of the most beautiful toy train sets ever made, and as far as Lionel collectors are concerned, second only to the State sets in desirability.

The first Blue Comet set Lionel ever made was jerry-rigged together in order to get a picture for the 1930 catalog. It differed considerably from the regular model that eventually came off the assembly line. The jerry-rigged first model was made from a combination of 309 series cars and State cars. A 309 car was first cut in half, then elongated by adding a piece to the middle, and then everything was soldered back together. Finally, the belly tanks from the State cars were cut down and placed on the elongated 309 cars. This resulted in a car that was longer than a 309 series, but shorter than a State car.

That prototype set is now in the possession of John Daniels of Pasadena, California, and it is easy to see the seams where the cars were soldered. In the 1931 catalog the Blue Comet was pictured the way it was produced; the differences between the set pictured in the 1931 catalog and the one pictured in 1930 are obvious.

The first Blue Comet set was pulled by a blue 390E. For the next year it was headed by a two-tone blue 400E. The cars were named after comets: two Pullmans, 420 Faye and 421 Westphal; and an observation, 442 Temple. The cars featured everything the State cars featured, but they were a little smaller. They were illuminated, had removable roofs, swivel seats, washrooms, six-wheel trucks and full trim. Another small difference between the Blue Comet and State cars is that on the State cars both the inner and outer doors in the lavatory are hinged. On the Comet only the outer door is hinged. The inner is fixed.

The observation car in the Blue Comet set had only one washroom and the cathedral windows at the end without the washroom are clear, not opaque.

The first Blue Comet cars had cast journals, brass trim, a darker shade of blue than later cars and dark blue diaphragms.

Brass journals replaced the cast in 1932 and a little later nickel journals replaced the brass and the shades of both blues became lighter. The diaphragms, however, remained dark blue.

The last and most sought-after version of the Blue Comet cars has nickel journals, nickel trim and the blues are all lighter than the early shades. The diaphragms were not painted dark blue.

Brass number plate with serif typeface.

Brass number plate with sans-serif typeface.

Blue Comet cars with combinations of the above characteristics turn up. For instance, there is a set with the early characteristics but with the diaphragms painted the lighter shade of blue. Also there is an early set with "Blue Comet" rubber stamped in black above the windows. This set is extremely rare.

The most valued Blue Comet set would be the late version with nickel trim headed by a 400E with nickel trim. The asking price for a set like this in like-new condition at a train meet in Pennsylvania in late 1976 was $3,500.

After the nickel-trimmed set would come the brass-trimmed sets headed by a 400E. Least valued would be the first version, headed by the 390E.

408E — apple green   419 Combination, 431 Diner, 418 Pullman, 490 Observation — apple green/red trim
408E — mojave   419 Combination, 431 Diner, 418 Pullman, 490 Observation — maroon/mojave/maroon trim
9 — dark green   429 Combination, 428 Pullman, 430 Observation — dark green/orange trim
9E — orange   429 Combination, 428 Pullman, 430 Observation — orange/apple green trim
380E — dark green   429 Combination — dark green/maroon trim

The Blue Comet was last cataloged in 1938 but the cars were offered separately through 1940 and perhaps even later, as Lionel kept selling Standard gauge until its inventories were exhausted.

424, 425, 426 SERIES "STEPHEN GIRARD" 1931-1938

The smallest and least detailed of Lionel's name sets was the so-called Stephen Girard. The cars were about six inches shorter than the State cars but they used the same six-wheel trucks. This resulted in a car with a rather truncated look to it, but the Girard cars are still very much in demand by collectors.

The cars were painted light green, with part of the roof painted dark green. The window trim was cream. The series consisted of the 424 Liberty Bell, 425 Stephen Girard, and 426 Coral Isle. The cars were orginally in a set called the Pennsylvania Limited by Lionel, but in 1935 the name was switched to the Broadway Limited. Once again, collectors have come to call these cars by a different name than Lionel ever did.

The real Broadway Limited, a crack Pennsylvania train, had many different cars through the years, including a "Liberty" series of baggage-club cars which included the Liberty Bell. There was also a series that had names of revolutionary figures, such as James Logan and Stephen Girard.

Girard was a Frenchman who came to America in 1776, started a shipping business and became an international trader and a prominent citizen of Philadelphia. He died in 1831, the richest man in the United States, and left $6,000,000 of his $7,000,000 estate to the city of Philadelphia to establish a school for orphans. The family of Girard hired Daniel Webster to challenge the will, but the Supreme Court ruled that Girard had a right to leave his money to the city, and in 1848 Girard College was opened.

The Coral Isle was a Pennsylvania car, too, but it never ran in the Broadway Limited. It ran for awhile as part of a "Spirit of St. Louis Limited."

The set of Lionel Girard cars was headed by 385, 390 or 392 steamers, or a matching two-tone green 9 electric. The set was cataloged from 1931 through 1938.

The early sets had brass trim and the later sets nickel. But the nameplates were always brass and the observation deck nickel on the late cars. The keystone on the back of the observation railing read "Pennsylvania Limited."

There was very little detail inside the cars, only a long bench on each side.

418, 419, 431, 490 SERIES 1923-1932

These were the first of the newly designed Classic era passenger cars. They were introduced in 1923 as the top-of-the-line set headed by the 402 and they remained the top-of-the-line set until 1929 when the State cars were introduced.

The cars made in 1923 and 1924 had the same 10 series trucks that were used on the large 10 series freight cars, and the 18, 19, 190 series held over from the early period.

The early cars were mojave with maroon window inserts, wood-grain doors, and were rubber-stamped "New York Central." The roof was held in with two knurled screws. The cars were illuminated and had a special pick-up assembly.

In 1925 they received their own six-wheel trucks with nickel journals. Maroon doors began to appear but the old wood-grain doors were still being used too, until their inventory was used up. A new illuminated observation deck was also added.

The 431 diner first appeared in 1927. It was included in a four-car set headed by a 408E. The catalog showed orange window inserts for the first time and the cars were rubber-stamped "Lionel Lines."

In 1929 the cars appeared in apple green for the first time. Mojave was also still available. In 1933, the year the cars were dropped, they came in a three-car set with a 400E steamer.

The apple green cars are worth more than the mojave, and the mojave cars with the six-wheel trucks are more valuable than the early cars with 10 series trucks.

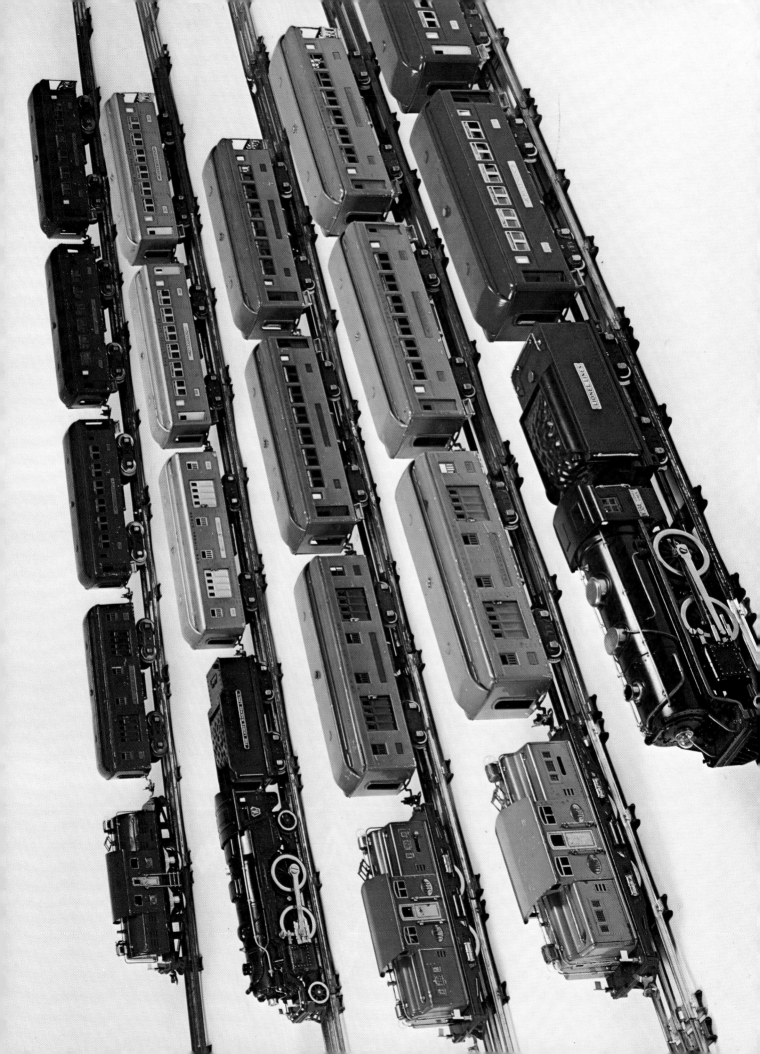

Interior trim included only swivel seats. The diner had tables and chairs which were closer to O gauge scale than Standard gauge. The diner did not appear until 1927 and the series came in many three-car sets which did not include the diner. Because of this, the 431 diner is the most valuable car in the series — worth probably three times as much as any other car. Some diners had hinged roofs.

There are no other production colors known except for the common apple green and the mojave. But there were some sets that came in such rare colors that there were probably only one or two of them made. These off-beat colors were probably paint samples. They include a gray set with red window trim that consisted of a 408E loco, and the 418, 419, 431 and 490 cars; a pink set with apple green window trim consisting of a 408E, 418, 419, and 490; a yellow cream set with red window trim and green doors consisting of a 408E, 418, 419, 431 and 490 cars, and a mustard set with red window trim consisting of a 402E loco and 418, 419 and 490 cars.

428, 429, 430 SERIES
1926-1930

This is an interesting series. It had the same bodies as the 418, 419, 490 series but came with four-wheel trucks instead of six-wheel trucks. They were made for a shorter period and are more highly prized. The four-wheel trucks employed by these cars are the same that were used on the 200 series freight cars.

The earliest cars made in the series were dark green with maroon window inserts. They came with both wood-grain and maroon doors. These cars were headed by a 380E with additional weight added to the frame. Later dark green cars with orange window trim came with the dark green 9.

The cars also come in orange with apple green trim and were headed by a matching 9 electric.

A number of highly sought-after uncataloged sets were also available. These were dark green, but came with orange trim rather than the maroon trim of the cataloged dark green cars. There were also 9s that headed these sets. A set headed by the big 381 was also uncataloged.

There is a very rare diner that goes with this series, too. It was never cataloged in a set, but they have turned up in both orange and dark green numbered 427 or 431. The 427 was available for separate sale.

319, 320, 322 SERIES
1924-1927
309, 310, 312 SERIES
1926-1940

The next two series of passenger cars are referred to as middle-sized. They measured a little longer than 13 inches and came in medium-priced sets.

The 319 series was introduced in 1924 and was only available through 1927. When headed by a 380 electric, the series came with 200 series trucks. When the series came with the lower 318 loco, they used 500 series trucks. The first year the cars came in three-car sets consisting of two 319 pullmans and an 322 observation with 100 series trucks. The next year the 320 baggage was added and the series came in four-car sets.

The cars came in maroon with mojave window trim and are commonly found rubber-stamped "New York Central." Less common are the cars with Illinois Central markings. The 320 came rubber-stamped "Lionel Electrical Railroad."

The 309, 310, 312 series was introduced in 1926 and was cataloged until 1940. Through the years it was available in a wide variety of different colors, some very attractive and desirable. The series was headed by the 318 and 9 electrics, and the 384, 390, 392 and 1835 steamers.

There was a two-car set which came in maroon with terra cotta roof and was headed by the 384.

The two-tone green set cataloged only in 1934 is the most difficult color combination to find. The set was headed by a gray 9E.

The second rarest color, two-tone blue, was also cataloged only in 1934. It was headed by an 1835E steamer.

Next in rarity would be the two-tone brown cars that collectors refer to as the Baby State set. These brown cars are more sought-after than the terra cotta and maroon combination, even

(left margin, rotated text)

380 Electric — maroon   322 Observation — maroon
1835E Steam loco, 1835W Tender — black   309 Pullman   312 Observation — light blue/aluminum
318 Electric — mojave   320 Baggage   312 Observation — mojave/maroon
318E Electric — pea green   310 Baggage   309 Pullman   312 Observation — pea green/orange
384 Steam loco, 384T Tender — black   2 319 Pullmans   310 Baggage   309 Pullman   312 Observation — maroon/terra cotta/cream

though the latter is harder to find. Other colors include blue and silver, mojave, and pea green. Pea green is the most common.

There is one set known to come in red with a silver roof. This was probably a paint sample.

All 319, 320, 322 series and early 309, 310, 312 cars had large windows in the vestibule doors. Late 309 series cars had small windows.

1766, 1767, 1768 SERIES
1934-1940

These cars were first made for Ives by Lionel. After the demise of Ives, they were cataloged with the regular Lionel line. The cars were handsome, were 16 inches long and had six-wheel trucks. Lionel also had a similar looking passenger series in their O-gauge line. For background information on how Lionel took over Ives, refer to the authors' book on prewar Lionel O gauge.

The 1766 baggage, 1767 pullman and 1768 observation were first cataloged by Lionel in 1934. The set was headed by a gray 385. The cars were painted terra cotta with a maroon roof. The trim was brass.

The difference between the Ives 1766 baggage car and Lionel's 1766 was the door. Ives doors were not embossed; Lionel's were. Both doors operated. The Ives car was rubber-stamped "Mail & Baggage" on the doors, while Lionel's had no rubber stamping.

In 1938 the cars came in a set headed by a gray 385. The paint scheme changed to red with maroon roof and the trim changed to nickel. On these nickel-trimmed cars the observation deck is painted aluminum. The only other Lionel observation with a painted deck is the blue and silver 312 observation.

The later red (vermilion) with maroon roof was made for a shorter time and is a little harder to find than the terra cotta version.

332, 337, 338 SERIES
1925-1932
and
332, 339, 341 SERIES

These two series are the smallest Standard gauge cars Lionel made. They came in low-priced sets headed by small locos such as the 8, 10, 384 and 390. The cars were 12 inches long, had 500 series trucks and came stamped

"Lionel Lines", "New York Central Lines" or "Illinois Central." A number of colors were available, they are all relatively common and prices are reasonable.

A new collector could get into Standard gauge with minimum financial strain by going after these passenger cars, the 500 series freights and the smaller steam and electric locos. The problem is that most collectors want a State Set or a Blue Comet almost immediately. The fun of collecting smaller, less ostentatious pieces is lost in the dash for the glamour items.

The difference in the two low-priced series has to do with the windows. The 337 and 338 cars have single windows. The 339 and 341 cars have paired windows. The 332 baggage was included in certain sets with both series.

The 337, 338 cars came in red with cream trim, mojave with maroon trim and the very common olive with maroon trim. Fewer mojave cars turn up than the others but all are considered common by collectors.

There were two rare Macy Special sets. One was red with cream trim and the other pea green with cream trim.

The 332, 339, 341 cars are found in gray with maroon trim, and peacock with orange trim. Least common would be the peacock version with dark green roof and orange trim. Some of these cars turn up with Ives decals applied over the Lionel rubber stampings. Also there is a very rare color known to exist. It has beige sides and maroon roof, doors and window trim. It is the same color as the O gauge Ives/Lionel 1965 series.

There are two very hard to find versions of the 332 baggage. One is a peacock baggage with orange trim and red doors that was cataloged in 1929 only. This was the first Lionel passenger car to come with red doors. Another unusual thing about the car was the divider. On the baggage with the red doors, the divider was also red. On all others, the divider was orange. The other rare version is an uncatalogued olive. It also had red doors.

RATING

The most desirable Lionel passenger sets are any of the known, legitimate color sample pieces. Then would come the State cars, followed by the Blue Comet set and the Stephen Girard set.

FREIGHT CARS

In the Early period the top of the line freight cars were the 10 series. They were introduced in 1907 and made through 1926. In 1926 Lionel introduced the 200 series freights, which replaced the 10 series and became the top-of-the-line-freight cars.

The lower priced freight cars in the Early period were called the 100 series. They were introduced in 1910 and also made through 1926. In 1927, Lionel introduced the 500 series freights, which were less expensive and smaller than the 200 series freights. They replaced the 100 series and became the less expensive freight cars.

There are some general characteristics of both 200 and 500 series freight cars. Most collectors break the cars into three categories: early cars (1926-1932), transition cars (1933-1936) and late cars (1937-1940).

The early cars have nickel journals, brass trim — by trim we mean ladders, handrails, plates, door handles and brakewheels — and are mostly painted dark colors.

The transition cars cover the change-over of the early cars with brass trim and the late cars with nickel trim. Transition cars can be identified by their copper journals and trim that is either all brass or a combination of brass and nickel.

The late cars are the easiest to spot. They have nickel journals and nickel trim and are painted bright colors. Occasionally a piece will turn up with a combination of brass and nickel trim. This would be a case of using up old inventories.

The nickel trim cars were made during a time when Lionel was selling mostly O gauge and Standard gauge was being phased out. Because of this, fewer late cars were sold and in most cases they are the most sought after and valuable version.

Another aid in establishing when a car was made is the brakewheel. The early cars had two-piece brakewheels made of brass. They were crimped and soldered with a cap in the center. The larger 200 series cars actually had a smaller brakewheel than the smaller 500 series during this time. The 200 series brakewheels were smaller in diameter.

Two-piece brakewheel.   One-piece brakewheel.

The transition cars had a one-piece brakewheel stamped in brass and the late cars had a one-piece brakewheel stamped in nickel.

Color helps, too. Collectors, with help from catalogs and private records, know the order in which various colors appeared. So, considering color, trim, journals and brakewheels, the year an item was made can be established with near certainty.

200 SERIES

The 1926 catalog showed both the old top-of-the-line freight cars (10 series) and the new top-of-the-line freight cars (200 series). The new cars had brass trim, nickel journals, and 200 series trucks, the same trucks that were used on the 428, 429, 430 series passenger cars. The new line of freight cars came with the best locos, like the 408E, 402 and 400E.

200 Series truck.

The cars are longer, bigger and higher than the less expensive 500 series. Only a few are difficult to find. Most are available and priced about the same as the postwar, plastic 6464 series cars.

We show the series in three color photographs. The first shows the early cars, the second the transition cars, and the third, the late nickel-trimmed cars. To have a complete collection of 200 series cars, a collector would have to acquire all the cars shown in the three photographs.

There are eleven cars in the series. Nine were introduced in 1926. The refrigerator car was introduced in 1929 and the floodlight car in 1931. Most of the cars were available through 1940. The hopper and the dump car were last cataloged in 1938.

211 FLATCAR

The flatcar came in only one color — black. All the versions had nickel stakes, although there have been distant rumors that there were some made with brass stakes. But no one has ever reported seeing one.

The flatcar was shown without a load in 1926, but in 1927 and after it came with a one-piece wood load, simulating individual planks. The bottom of the load was drilled out so the wood would rest solidly above the coupler pins that protruded through the frame.

The wood load also had notches on the side so it locked around the base of the stakes, preventing shifting.

212 GONDOLA

The gondola was made in gray, maroon and green. Maroon is the most common color. It is known to exist with both serif and non-serif lettering. The serif lettering came in both normal and bold-face.

Special LCL, or Less Than Carload, containers were designed for the gondola. They were sold separately and three fit perfectly on the car. When the gondola came with a work train the load consisted of barrels and a tool chest.

The 212 gondola is an exception to the rule that late cars are the most difficult to find. The first 212s were painted gray, but only for a very short time. Therefore the gray is now the most difficult version to find and the most sought after.

Early serif typeface.

Transitional sans- serif typeface.

Late serif typeface.

The gondola was made in a number of non-regular production colors. Known to exist are a medium green, mojave and a dark green which is shown on opposite page. These, like all other special-run items, are extremely rare.

200 Series — Early
212 Gondola — gray with 208 tool chest and barrels
211 Flat — black
214R Refrigerator — ivory/peacock
217 Caboose — orange/maroon
212 Gondola — dark green (very rare)
215 Tank — pea green
216 Hopper — dark green
214 Boxcar — terra cotta/dark green
213 Cattle — mojave/maroon
219 Derrick — peacock/dark green/red boom without red window trim
218 Dump — mojave (two controls)

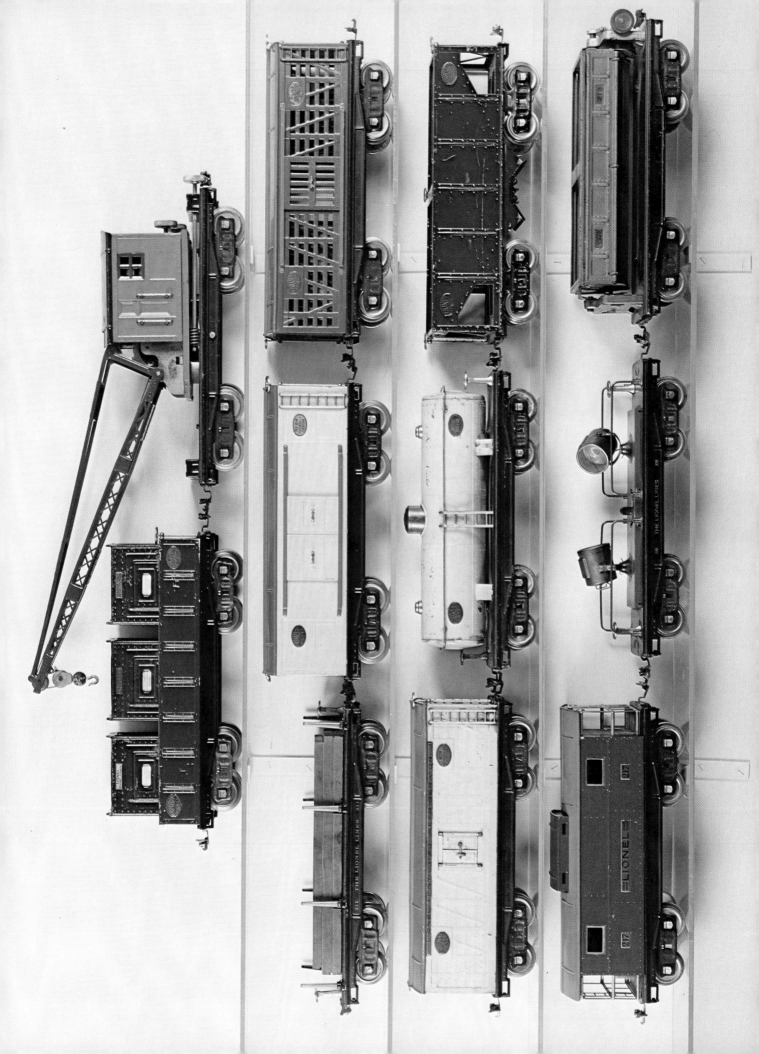

205 L.C.L. container with abandoned prototype outside the engine house at Croton-Harmon yards.

213 CATTLE

The first of the cattle cars was mojave with a maroon roof. Later it came in an unusual but attractive terra cotta and maroon combination; a terra cotta and pea green; and a cream with maroon roof and nickel trim.

The most common color is the terra cotta with the pea green roof. The most difficult to find — and among the most difficult to find in the entire series — is the late cream and maroon combination.

214 BOXCAR

First made in terra cotta and dark green, then cream and orange, and finally yellow and brown, this car is close to the late cattle cars in value but is a little easier to find, with an exception. For some reason the early boxcar is harder to find than the early cattle car. Some of the late boxcars turn up with a combination of both nickel and brass trim.

214R REFRIGERATOR

This is the only car in the series never cataloged in sets. It first appeared painted ivory with a peacock roof. The late version, painted white and light blue, is the second most difficult car to find in the series. It is known to exist with both nickel and brass plates. The nickel plate version is more desirable but both versions are hard to find and highly prized.

Many refrigerator cars turn up with a combination of brass and nickel plates.

215 TANK

The early car was pea green with red inking on the brass plates. Next, the tanker came in ivory with or without the Sunoco decal. This second version exists with red-inked plates, black-inked plates, or a mixture.

The last regular production car was aluminum with a Sunoco decal. This car comes with both nickel trim and a nickel handrail and with brass trim and a copper handrail.

The aluminum tanker with the nickel trim is worth a bit more than the same car with brass trim. Next in worth is the white with the Sunoco decal. The most common is the early pea green version. Also cataloged but not known to exist is a 215 in orange with Shell decals.

216 HOPPER

This car was made in one color — dark green. It is not hard to find in the early and transition versions, but the late nickel version is the hardest car to find in the entire series.

The bottom opened, allowing the load to be emptied. This hopper never came with a simulated coal load, as the 516 hopper did, but artificial coal was available.

One reason the nickel version is so rare is that it was last cataloged in 1938.

217 CABOOSE

The early 217 was orange with a maroon roof. The number and name plates were painted maroon rather than the normal brass plates. Lettering on the painted plates was gold.

The transitional 217 caboose was red with a peacock roof and brass trim. The cupola was painted either red or peacock. Peacock is harder to find. A one-of-a-kind variation is known in pea green with a red roof.

The late 217 was painted light red with a red roof and nickel trim.

The most sought-after 517 is the early version painted orange with a maroon roof. Next would be the late version.

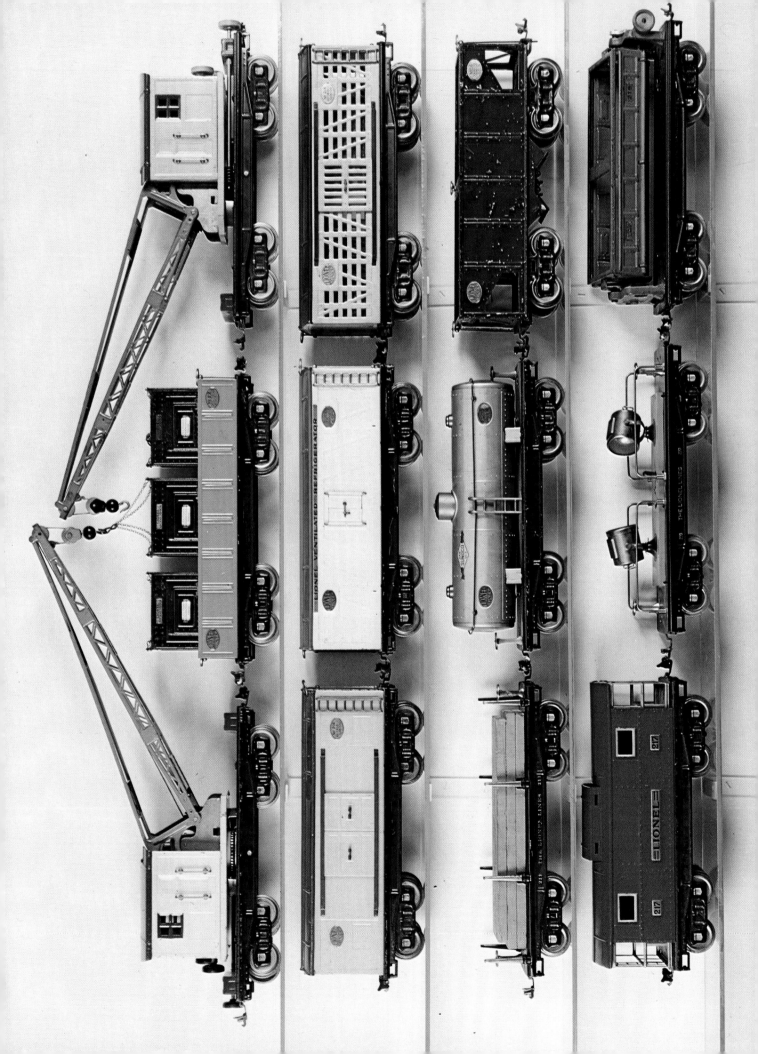

218 DUMP

This was a popular car because it had what Joshua Cowen liked to call "action." The dumping bin was controlled by a knob at one end. When the knob was turned, the bin would tilt and the side would open, releasing the load. This action was accomplished through a "worm and gear" mechanism.

The regular production dump car was mojave. The car is a good example how quality diminished as time went on. The earliest models had two brass knobs and die-cast gears. The next car had one brass knob and Bakolite gears. These gears are often decayed and replacement gears are available. Both these cars had brass ends. The last version of the car didn't even have brass ends. It had painted, stamped-metal ends and one knob. So over the years the dump cars lost brass knobs, gears and brass ends.

| 218 Dump car with two knobs. | 218 Dump car with single knob. |

By cutting corners and costs Lionel could maintain the price of an item over a long period of time.

There are some very rare limited-production versions around. One, shown in the 1926 catalog, is green with red ends. Also in the hands of collectors are a gray with brass ends and a pea green with maroon ends.

There is no late, nickel version of the dump. It was last cataloged in 1938. The early version with two knobs is probably the hardest to find but the car sold well and is common. But because kids played so much with it, it is hard to find in good condition.

219 CRANE

This was another extremely popular car. It was always given a lot of space in the catalog and was pictured attractively. The thing was huge. Kids could do all sorts of things with it.

The first cranes were peacock green with a red boom and unpainted windows. Lionel thought this was a little drab and soon started painting the windows red. This was not additional window trim but simply a case of the cab being masked, and red paint sprayed on. The red on the window matched the red boom.

The next crane came in yellow with a red roof and green boom. The last version was ivory with a red roof and green boom. Some of these later cranes also came with the booms painted the same red as the roof.

A rare forward window version was made and is shown in the 1928 and 1929 catalog.

The early cranes came with brass hooks. Later versions had nickel hooks.

The crane cab could be turned, the boom moved up and down, and the hook raised and lowered. This was done by means of three control knobs at the rear of the car. On the first cranes the knobs were brass, then they were nickeled, then blackened pot metal. These die-cast pot metal knobs broke easily.

The yellow crane is found with all three types of knobs, the white version with only the die-cast knobs.

The most valuable crane is the ivory with red roof, followed by the yellow with red roof. The early peacock is the most common.

220 FLOODLIGHT

First cataloged in 1931, this was the last 200 series car to be introduced.

The early car was terra cotta with brass lights and most of the early cars had the brakewheel on the left. The late version, painted green with lights, had the brakewheel on the right most of the time. The floodlights are the same ones used on the O gauge floodlight car.

The nickel version is harder to find and more valuable. Both versions, however, are pretty easy to find.

RATING

The late hopper is the hardest car to find in the series. Next are the late full-nickel versions of the refrigerator, cattle and boxcars. These are followed by the early refrigerator car, the white crane and the early caboose.

After these there is a big drop off in value and a big increase in availability. Others in the 200 series are about equal in availability.

500 SERIES

512 Gondola —
  peacock

516 Hopper —
  red

513 Cattle —
  olive green/
  orange

514 Box —
  cream/orange

This series replaced the early 100 series and is a good place for the new collector to start. There are about forty collectable variations and of these, only four can be considered hard to find or expensive. The rest are all readily available. The average price of the Standard gauge 500 series cars is lower than the average price of the postwar 6464-series cars.

The main difference between the 200 series and the 500 series is size and price. The 200 series is bigger and more expensive. The 500 series used the same trucks as the 330 series passenger cars and featured the same amount of trim as the more expensive 200 series cars.

515 Tank —
  terra cotta

514 Refrigerator
  — ivory/
  peacock

All the cars were cataloged in sets and were usually headed by such locos as the 385E, 1835E and 10.

There were 10 cars in the series. Six were introduced in 1927. The hopper came out in 1928; the 514R refrigerator and 514 box in 1929, and the floodlight car in 1931. The cars featured all-metal construction, bright colors, brass or nickel trim, journals, nameplates and number plates.

517 Caboose —
  pea green/red

511 Flat —
  dark green

Each car came in the same three basic versions as the 200 series — the early, transition and late — and the same general characteristics apply.

Early 500 series truck.

Late 500 series truck.

511 FLAT CAR
1927-1939

The flat car came in two colors. The first was dark green. This version had nickel stakes, nickel journals and gold rubber-stamped lettering. The dark green car also exists with copper journals.

The late version was painted medium green with nickel trim. This car is known to exist with both silver and gold rubber-stamped lettering. The silver is harder to find.

The early cars had a single-piece wood load, similar to the one that came with the 211 flat car. Later cars came with individual pieces of

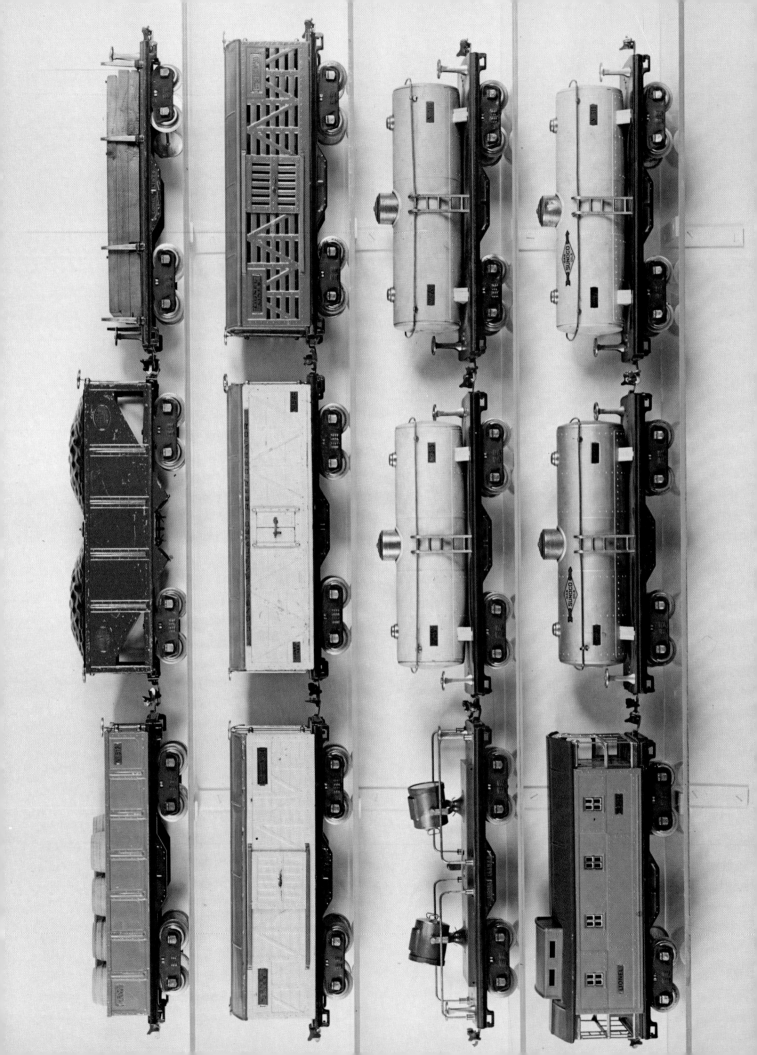

wood. The early cars also came with the brake-wheel on the left, later cars with it on the right. The nickel version is harder to find.

512 GONDOLA
1927-1940

The gondola came first in peacock, then in green. The late green version is harder to find. The early cars came with curved wine-type barrels, later cars with drum-type barrels. The 512 gondola is extremely common.

513 CATTLE CAR
1927-1938

The first version of the cattle car was olive green with an orange roof. It was made for a very short time. The second version was painted orange with a pea green roof. It is the one that is the most common.

The last version — painted cream with a maroon roof and nickel trim — is the second hardest car to find in the series.

Lionel must have ordered orange paint by the thousands of gallons. It appears more frequently on more different items than any other color.

514 BOXCAR
1929-1940

Most collectors feel only two versions of the boxcar were made — the early cream with an orange roof and the late yellow with a brown roof. But some collectors feel Lionel also made a cream version with a green roof. The reason for doubt over the cream version is that it would be easy to take the door guides and roof from a cattle car and put them on a cream box-car. Therefore, most collectors do not accept this color as a legitimate variation.

The late yellow and brown combination is by far the most difficult to find and the most sought after by collectors.

One collector who *does* think Lionel made the cream boxcar with the green roof is Dave Christiansen of Hammond, Indiana. Dave says he bought one from a private citizen and the car did not appear tampered with.

REFRIGERATOR CAR
514 1927, 28
514R 1929-1940

When the first refrigerator car appeared in 1927, it was designated 514 and painted ivory with a peacock roof. It ran the same way in 1928, but in 1929 an R was added and it remained 514R the rest of its run.

The color remained ivory with a peacock roof until the late version appeared in 1937. This was the rare nickel variation and painted white with a light blue roof. It is one of the rarest cars in the series.

Even though the 514 in ivory and peacock was only made for two years, it seems more cars turn up with 514 plates than 514R plates.

515 TANK
1927-1940

The 515 tank first appeared in terra cotta. Next it came in ivory, with or without the Sunoco decal. Most of the late cars were aluminum with a Sunoco decal, except for the highly-prized Shell tank car in orange.

The Shell tank car is considered to be the most difficult of all the 500 series to find and as prized as the 216 with nickel trim. These two cars are the hardest to find of all the Classic period freights — excluding one-of-a-kind color samples.

This was another car with a brakewheel that was placed differently through the years. The early terra cotta cars had the wheel on the left, while the later cars came with the brake-wheel either on the left or right side.

500 SERIES — TRANSITIONAL CARS
512 Gondola — peacock   511 Flat — dark green
514 Box — cream/orange   513 Cattle — orange/pea green
520 Floodlight — orange   514R Refrigerator — ivory/peacock
517 Caboose — pea green/red   515 Tank —
516 Hopper — red   515 Tank —
                                 515 Tank — tan w/Sunoco decal
515 Tank — ivory w/Sunoco decal

87

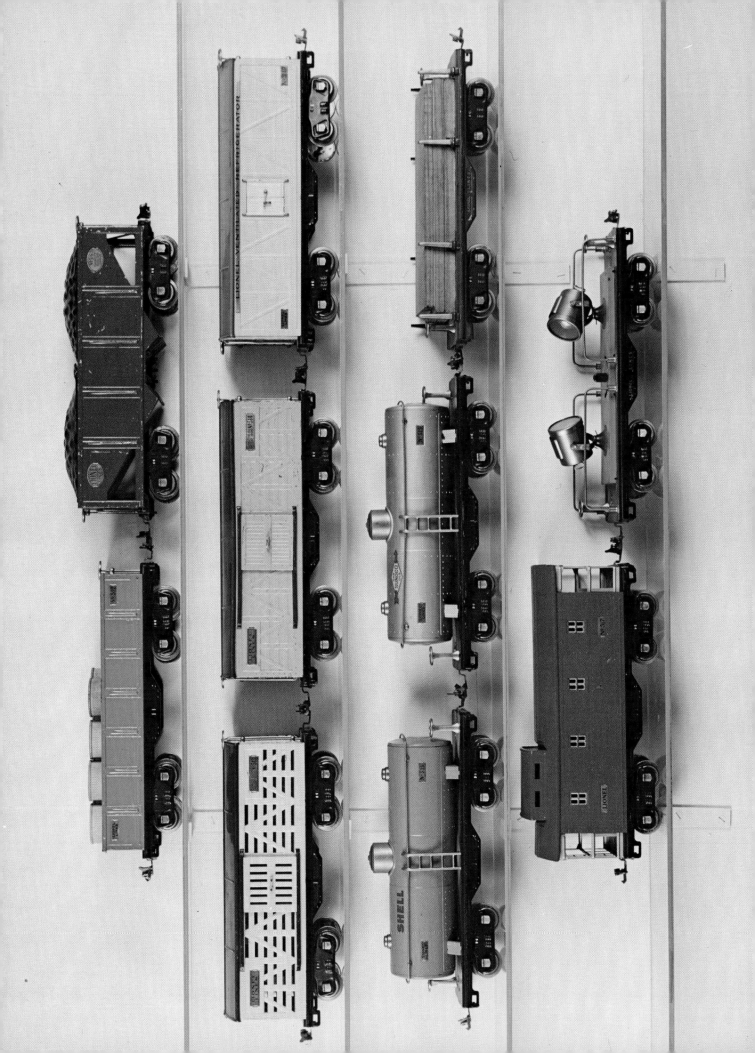

We normally would call the orange tank car "rare" but after writing about knobbed-roof passenger cars, trolleys, and some other early pieces, we had better stick with "prized" and "hard-to-find."

516 HOPPER
1928-1940

The hopper was made only in red. It came with and without the simulated coal piles.

A very sought-after set consisted of a black 318E, three hoppers and the prized red and black caboose. This set was known as the Coal Train and is shown on page 76.

Some hoppers have black rubber-stamped capacity data on the side.

The rarest hopper is the late nickel version. The early brass version is the most common. The one with the rubber stamped lettering is easier to find than the nickel version but harder than the early brass version.

520 FLOODLIGHT CAR
1931-1940

The floodlight car first appeared painted with a terra cotta base and brass floodlights. The floodlights were the same ones that were used on the O gauge floodlight car.

The late version of the floodlight had a green base with nickel lights.

Both versions are common as the car sold very well. Of the two, the nickel version is more difficult to find.

The brakewheel shifted sides on this car as it did on the flat and tank cars. The early cars had it on the left; the late cars had it on either side but mostly on the right.

517 CABOOSE
1927-1940

Like most cabooses, the 517 is very common. Every freight train needs a caboose and Lionel sold a lot of freight trains. The first and most common version was painted green with a red roof. It came with both orange window trim and brass window trim.

The late caboose was all red with nickel trim. The ends were painted silver on this nickel version.

The most desirable 517 caboose is the one that came with the Coal Train. It was red with a black roof and was not sold seperately.

RATING

By far the most sought-after car in the 500 series is the 515 orange Shell tank car. Next would come the black and red 517 caboose, followed by the late (nickel trim) versions of the 513 cattle, 514R reefer and the 516 hopper with rubber-stamped lettering on the sides.

517 Caboose.

500 Series — Late
512 Gondola — green
513 Cattle — cream/maroon
515 Tank — orange
517 Caboose — red
516 Hopper — red
514 Box — yellow/brown
515 Tank — aluminum
520 Floodlight — green
511 Flat — medium green
514R Refrigerator — white/light blue

89

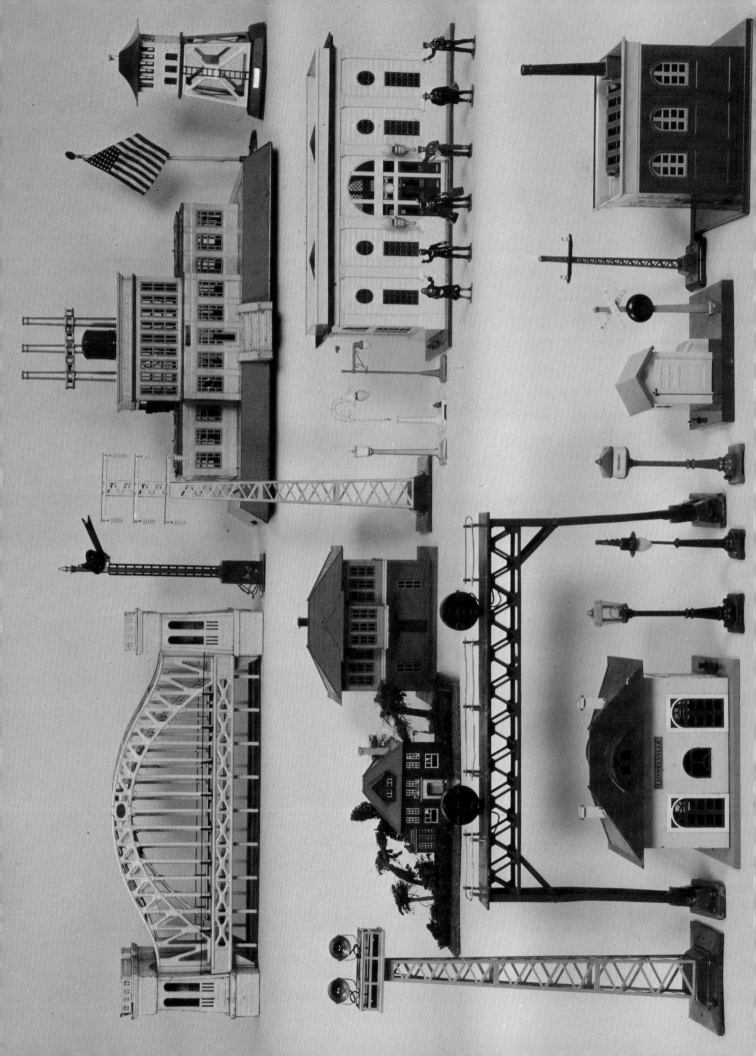

ACCESSORIES

ACCESSORIES
300 Hellgate Bridge   80 Semaphore   840 Industrial Power Station
911 Country Estate   437 Switch Signal Tower   94 High Line Tower
92 Floodlight Tower   0440 Twin Signal Bridge   126 Station   Nos. 56, 58, 57

90 Flag Staff   438 Signal Tower   550 Miniature Railroad figures
Nos. 35, 58, 64   Street Lamps   116 Station   463 Power Station
Street Lamps   76 Warning Bell and Shack   060 Telegraph Post

When it came to its Standard gauge accessories, Lionel seemed unconcerned with accurate size or realistic color combinations. Emphasis was placed instead on the play value of an item and on bright colors, whether the colors were representative of a prototype or not.

There were many accessories that were sold for use with both O and Standard gauge trains, and that in itself precluded accurate scale reproduction. The accessories were simply toys, and they were toys that were meant to be played with.

Some Standard gauge accessories that were sold with O gauge trains were discussed in the authors' book on prewar O gauge (Volume I).

Lionel salesmen counted heavily on accessories to increase business during the slow time of the year, which was anytime other than Christmas. Lionel like any other toy company, did 75 per cent of its total business the last three months of the year. By the late 1930s accessories represented about 25 per cent of

Lionel's total sales, and much of that came during the slack months.

Generally, early accessories, those made before 1936, had brass trim and were painted green, cream and terra cotta. Later accessories had nickel trim and were painted cream, red and silver. In most cases the later colors are harder to find.

The photographs in this section of the large Standard gauge layout on which a great many accessories can be seen, were taken at the Lionel Antique Train and Seashell Museum in Sarasota, Florida.

444 ROUNDHOUSE SECTION
1932-1934

This was a very large, expensive and gaudy accessory. For those reasons, and also because it was available for only three years, it is the most valuable accessory Lionel ever made. At 1977 prices one section was worth about $1,500.

5 444 roundhouse sections, 435 power house, 195 Lionel village and 200 turntable.

Roundhouse sections were designed to be connected to each other. The maximum number you could connect was eight but that would make a complete circle with no entrance, so seven was the sensible maximum.

The roundhouse sections were a bit misdesigned. The sections were not big enough. Only the smallest Standard gauge loco could fit inside without sticking out.

Even less practical was the 200 turntable that was designed to go with the roundhouse. The turntable wasn't big enough to hold even the smallest steam loco with its tender. Electrics were the only engines that would fit and electrics didn't use roundhouses.

Roundhouse sections are known to exist only in their early colors: terra cotta, cream and pea green. The 200 turntable came in two combinations: the early red and green, which is common; and the late red and black, which is very hard to find. Few collectors know how rare this late combination is, and those who do don't seem to care much. The 200 turntable has never caused much excitement among collectors.

840 POWER STATION
1928-1942

This was another large and very imposing accessory. It is known to exist only in the early colors: green base, cream sides and terra cotta roof. There have been reports of one existing in the late colors — white with a red roof — but none of the reports have been verified. The one pictured is repainted.

The power station came with a number of small parts, such as steps, smokestacks and a water tower, but when the station is found now these small parts are usually missing.

435 POWER STATION
1926-1938

This little power station is harder to find than the 840 power station but is worth only a fraction of the value of the 840. The 435 had cream sides with a terra cotta roof and one smokestack.

155 freight sheds, 840 power station, 911, 912, 913 scenic plots and 145 double station.

LIONEL VILLAGES

The largest of the Lionel villages was the 921. It was divided into three sections and was more than six feet long. The end sections had a curving base, while the center section had a straight base. The sections were landscaped, with trees, shrubbery and grass interlacing the bungalows and villas.

The villages were made of wood and cardboard and were easily damaged. The center section is the most difficult of the sections to find.

A smaller version, the 920, was also made. It was comprised of the two curved end sections only.

SCENIC PLOTS

These were smaller landscaped sections that came with one, two or three Lionel houses. The houses sat on a wood platform that was covered with simulated grass, shrubbery and trees. The largest of the plots was the 195 terrace. Other plot numbers were 911, 912 and 913. They are shown in the background in the photograph on page 98.

184 BUNGALOW, 191 VILLA & 189 VILLA

These were the three basic designs of the house used on the plots and villages. The houses came in many different colors and in many different versions. Some had dormers and some did not; some had entranceways and others did not. Most that turn up are lithographed. The very early ones were hand-painted, and are very hard to find.

The houses were attractive and well-made, but they were tiny, closer to HO gauge than anything else.

921 Lionel scenic park, 912 scenic plot, 428 switch tower.

840 power station (late colors — repainted), 915 curved tunnel (foreground), 140 curved tunnel (background), 94 high tension towers and 63 double light poles.

140L AND 915 TUNNELS

Lionel made many different tunnels over the years, but the two largest and most valuable are the 140L, curved, which was made of lightweight brass, and the 915, which was made of pressed felt. Both are hard to find in good condition because they were fragile. The 140L is the higher of the two at 20 inches, but the 915 is longer, 65 inches.

The brass 140L is more in demand.

94 HIGH TENSION TOWER
1932-1942

This was a good model, although it did not sell well. It is much in demand today. The early colors were gray and maroon. The later colors were red and silver. The early colors are harder to find.

The tower came with six hanging insulators and was 20-inches high.

92 FLOODLIGHT

The floodlight tower was also 20 inches high. It had two floodlights on the top. It came first painted green and terra cotta and later painted red and silver. The early color combination is harder to find.

300 HELLGATE BRIDGE

This was a wonderful model of the bridge that spans the East River in New York. The currents were so treacherous around that section of the Hudson that ancient Dutch sailors called the area the "Gates of Hell." When the bridge was erected over that same area it was called, not surprisingly, the Hellgate Bridge.

Lionel's model was sturdy and came in both the early and late colors, the late being more desirable.

A "double" Hellgate Bridge can be made by removing one of the portals and joining two bridges.

Hellgate railroad bridge, the longest railroad bridge in the world when it was built, spanning New York City's East River from the borough of Queens to Ward's Island in the East River, where these photos were taken.

116 DOUBLE STATION
1931-1934

This station is much in demand and is one of the few accessories where the early colors are harder to find than the later colors. The early version had cream sides, green trim with a tan base. The late version was painted cream with a red trim and base. The 116 was basically the same station as the 115 illuminated station but about 25 percent bigger.

441 WEIGHING SCALE

From the 1934 Lionel catalog: "You can actually weigh your model freight. There is a real beam scale accurately calibrated so you can weigh all your rolling stock by running it on the specially constructed track platform. An assortment of various weights are included. The base and scale housing are made of steel, with rich enamel finish. The weighing house is illuminated."

The beam of the scale was made of die-cast metal and when found today is usually broken or severely warped. The little brass weights are usually missing.

STREET LAMPS

Lionel made lots of street lamps and many of them were modeled after actual street lights in the New York City area. The photographs in this section show Lionel models with their prototypes in the background.

A favorite with collectors is the 57 lamp post that is shown above against a background of neon lights at 42nd and Broadway. The 57 lamp post is usually found in orange but also exists in yellow or gray. Most say "Broadway" on two sides and "Main" on the other two sides. But a few say "42nd" on two sides and "Main" on the other two sides.

The most difficult street lamp to find is the 52. It stood 14 inches high, was painted aluminum and had two lights at the top. It was available from 1933 through 1941.

RATING

The most valued of all Lionel Standard gauge accessories is the 444 roundhouse section. Next would come the 840 power station, the large villages, the large tunnels, the 116 double station, and the 300 Hellgate Bridge.

441 Weighing station.

61 lamp post with its prototype on W. 17 Street off of Fifth Avenue in New York, nine blocks from the former Lionel office on E. 26 Street. Only a handful of these cast iron lamp posts remain, saved from destruction by a Landmarks Preservation group.

67 lamp post with its prototype at the intersection of Broadway and Fifth Avenue on 23 Street in New York, within actual sight of the Lionel building on E. 26 Street. The Toy Building is located at this corner, where the annual toy fairs were held and new Lionel products were unveiled. MPC now has offices, a showroom and an operating layout in this building on Fifth Avenue. Rising in the background is the Empire State Building.

57 lamp post ("Broadway" and "Main Street") in the middle of New York's theatre district on Broadway in the Times Square area. Theatre marquees and neon advertising signs in the background while traffic passes.

116 "Lionel City" station with its prototype, Grand Central Terminal, in the background. Grand Central was completed in 1913 with its two levels on the site of an earlier depot built by Commodore Cornelius Vanderbilt in 1871.

97

OO GAUGE

During the 1930s there were a number of American companies making OO gauge trains, most of them in kit form for the serious modeler. Probably the best known of the companies were Scalecraft of Chicago and Nason of Philadelphia, both of them tiny compared to Lionel or American Flyer. Other companies making OO included Star Lines, Amity, and Famco Models.

At this time OO was probably more popular with model builders than HO gauge, although HO had come on the scene somewhat sooner. Bing, the German manufacturer, brought out the first HO trains in 1924. The difference in the two gauges is only an eighth of an inch — OO measures ¾-inch between the rails and HO gauge ⅝ — but Elliott Donnelley, the owner of Scalecraft, explained why he preferred to manufacture OO gauge: "I experimented with both an HO model and an OO model before deciding which to produce. I found out that at that time there wasn't a good enough motor that was small enough to use in HO. So I went into OO, which was a little bigger. There was a good motor on the market that fit nicely into my OO models."

That was in 1936. Lionel decided to break into the OO market in 1938, when they came out with a scale Hudson and four scale freight cars. They were fine models, but Donnelley always maintained Lionel's first cars were, as they say in the design business, "knock-offs." Donnelley said Lionel merely assembled some of Scalecraft's models, put Lionel decals on them, and offered them as samples to stores while they were having dies made of Scalecraft parts.

"Lionel's freight cars were the same as mine," Donnelley said a short time before his death in 1976. "As a matter of fact, the first samples they sent out were actually my cars.

Scalecraft hopper.

Lionel hopper.

"I happened to be walking down Fifth Avenue in New York and I looked into F.A.O. Schwartz's window and they had a big display of Lionel OO gauge. I went in to see the buyer whom I had been trying to sell for a long time and he started to tell me what a wonderful line Lionel had.

"I said, 'That's fine, but those are all my cars in the window.'

"He said, 'What do you mean your cars? Those are Lionel's.'

"I said, 'Come on with me.'

"So he came down with me to the window and I took the cars out and every car said 'Scalecraft' on the bottom. Lionel couldn't get their line out for Christmas, so they used mine as samples to sell from and then made their cars almost exactly like mine.

"I had the patent on the miniature truck suspensions that I was using on my OO freight cars. Lionel not only copied the suspension but copied the cars. And they did it without my permission, so my lawyers contacted Lionel and told them about the infringement.

"From that time on Lionel paid me a royalty."

And from that time on Lionel dominated the OO market, at least until World War II started and toy production was halted.

"I couldn't compete," said Donnelley. "In fact, I kind of got discouraged and decided to sell the business . . . but then the war came along and the government wouldn't let us make toys anyway and I got into war work, making 50-calibre and 30-calibre bullet draw-dies. I started out with what I thought was an order for $7,800, but I read it wrong. The order was for $780,000. I went from 25 employees to 450 employees in six weeks."

After the war Donnelley finally did sell Scalecraft, but he never lost his interest in modeling. At the time of his death three decades later, his estate in Lake Forest, Illinois, contained four miles of winding 1½-inch scale railroad on which he ran live model steam engines. There was a full-sized passenger depot and a work shed on the grounds, and the place served as headquarters for a railroad club of about 50 members. Sitting behind the station was a large green locomotive that had been used in the movie "Around the World in 80 Days." It had cost Donnelley, a member of a well-known Midwestern publishing family, $20,000 just to have it shipped from India to Lake Forest.

Lionel, after the war, did not get out of the toy business, of course, but they did get out of OO. Just why they did is an interesting question.

Between 1938 and 1942 the Lionel OO line sold well and the product was good — even if, as claimed with some evidence by Elliott Donnelley, the line's origin was somewhat suspicious. The cars were made entirely of cast metal. There was no Bakelite from which paint would flake, as there was on some O gauge cars. The OO gauge Hudson was just as good as the great O gauge version and was offered in both a full- and semi-detailed versions. The locos also ran well.

Because Lionel had such a good start in OO gauge, many collectors feel the company should have expanded the line after the war. This probably would have prevented other manufacturers from getting such a foothold in HO production. But Lionel had other considerations in 1946.

Even though their OO line had sold well, Lionel's O gauge still represented by far the largest percentage of its sales. This was the line on which Joshua Cowen decided to expend most of Lionel's efforts in the postwar battle with American Flyer for prominence in the toy train field. Flyer had made the decision to abandon O gauge for a handsome line of S gauge (⅞-inch between rails). To counteract this, Lionel was hard at work developing such things as the turbine and GG-1, perfecting smoke and the knuckle couple, and planning new diesels and operating cars. And they wanted to bring these things out in the gauge that was their strength — O gauge.

Thus, the discontinuation of OO gauge and some of the nicest pieces the company ever made. It was a decision the company would live to regret, but it made sense at the time.

The scale OO gauge Hudson, which came out in 1938 and was as fully detailed as the O gauge 5344, was numbered 001E. Its tender was numbered 001T and came with or without a whistle. The engine and tender were die-cast, except for the coal pile on the tender, which was Bakelite.

The freight cars were all scale and die-cast, too, and consisted of 0014 yellow boxcar, 0015 silver Sunoco tank car, 0016 gray hopper with Southern Pacific markings, and 0017 red caboose with Lionel markings.

In 1939 the double-O line was expanded to include full- and semi-scale sets, and sets for both two- and three-rail track. That meant a total of four locos: the 001E, full-scale, running on three rails; the 002E, semi-scale, running on three rails; the 003E, full-scale, running on two rails; and the 004E, semi-scale, running on two rails.

Detailed 001E.

Modified 002E.

The 001E pulled the same tender and cars as it had in 1938, but the colors changed. The boxcar was now tuscan, the tanker was black with Shell markings, and the hopper was black. The caboose was again red but the markings changed from "Lionel Lines" to "N.Y.C."

The 002 and its tender pulled an 0024 boxcar in tuscan, 0025 tanker in black and 0027 caboose in red. The 003 led a set with 0044 boxcar, 0045 tanker, 0046 coal and 0047 caboose. The 004 came with 0074 boxcar, 0075 tanker and 0077 caboose. The color of the cars with the 003 and 004 were the same as with the 001 and 002.

Scale 001T.   Modified 002T.

The full-scale locos had more valve gear and piping detail than the semi-scale versions, plus a front coupler that was missing on the semi-scale. These were the same differences that distinguished the 700E O gauge Hudson from the 763E. All the Hudsons, full- and semi-

scale were stamped with the number 5342 under the cab window; "New York Central" was stamped on the tenders.

The reverse unit used in the OO gauge Hudsons was the same unit that Lionel used in their scale switchers.

There were two methods used to attach the loco to the tender. In 1938 the 001E used a drop pin and a chain. This was the same method used on the 700E. In 1939 Lionel switched to a spring-held pin assembly and this method was used through 1942.

All the OO gauge tenders were offered with or without a whistle.

Scale 0017.

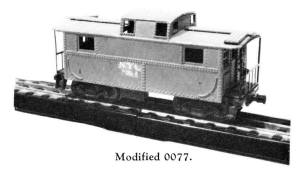

Modified 0077.

Scalecraft caboose.

There wasn't much difference between the full-scale and semi-scale cars, either. For instance, the semi-scale caboose lacked only the smokestack that was present on the full-scale model. And on the semi-scale boxcar only the brake cylinder was missing.

101

All the same sets were offered again in 1940, '41 and '42. The 001E loco and 40-series freights were offered in kit form.

Switches and crossovers were available in the three-rail versions in 1938 only. None were made for two-rail operation. Those three-rail switches and crossovers are hard to find.

OO freight cars "new in the box".

Generally, the two-rail track was temperamental. The sections came apart easily and were dependable only when soldered together. The OO gauge three-rail tracks clipped together and were relatively trouble-free. The diameter of two-rail track was 42-inches, while the diameter of the three-rail was 27-inches.

RATING

Both semi-scale versions of the loco 002 and 004 are harder to find than the scale versions. The hardest to find of the four is the 002, three-railer.

The freight cars made in 1938 only are the hardest of the double-O cars to find. The black hopper, which was not included in semi-scale sets, is also hard to find. The rest of the freight cars are about equal in availability.

The 1941 catalog pictured some unusual items, including a hopper with Reading markings instead of the normal Southern Pacific, and a black Sunoco tank instead of the usual Shell. None of these items are known to exist.

Lionel's OO gauge is an open area for collectors. All the items are available, and a complete collection could be put together for about $600.

1940 catalog page covering OO gauge

HO GAUGE

In the years immediately following World War II it looked as if Lionel had made the right decision by deciding to concentrate on their O gauge line and drop OO. Their sales quickly outdistanced those of what they perceived as their main competitor, American Flyer, which was selling S gauge.

Lionel had a corner on the postwar O-gauge market, had introduced their diesels, including the highly successful F-3, and, when 1953 ended, could report the highest sales in their history, more than $32 million.

But irresistibly a change was taking place in the buying pattern of American train customers. The change was slow at first, but steadily increased in the postwar years: people were buying smaller trains, especially HO gauge.

Much of this change had to do with space. There just wasn't as much of it in the postwar boom years as there had been before the war. A population explosion was taking place; more people were living in apartments and in houses with smaller rooms; and there were just more people than in the old days. The small HO gauge was suitable for this style of living and one company after another began manufacturing it. None of these companies was as big as Lionel, and Lionel at first did not notice the inroads HO was making because in those postwar boom years there seemed to be enough business for everyone. But by the mid-1950s the combined sales of these HO manufacturers had exceeded Lionel's O gauge sales.

Had Lionel chosen to stay in the OO market, of course, they would have been in a position to meet the demand for smaller trains and probably could have deflected the advance of HO. But they didn't. And after the zenith year of 1953, Lionel business began to sink. In 1956 sales were down to $22 million — and dropping. Lionel decided to go into HO gauge.

They contacted Rivarossi, an Italian manufacturer known for making high-quality HO gauge trains. The two firms entered an agreement: Rivarossi would make the trains and Lionel would distribute them under the Lionel name and pay a percentage to Rivarossi. Lionel was thus spared the expense of making their own HO dies, while Rivarossi, which was not well-known in this country, was assured of getting more distribution through the biggest toy train maker in the United States than they ever could on their own.

Lionel announced their first HO gauge trains in a two-page folder they distributed with their regular 1957 catalog. The line did not appear in the catalog itself.

1957

The Rivarossi line was a good one. All the items were well-made and handsome, particularly the boxcars. 1957 was the only year that Lionel acknowledged that someone else was making their HO line. The special folder that went with the catalog gave Rivarossi's name, and all the cars were stamped "Rivarossi" on the bottom.

The items offered in HO followed closely Lionel's O gauge line. Boxcars had such familiar markings as NYC Pacemaker, Rutland, Minneapolis & St. Louis, New Haven, Timken and Sentinel. Fairbanks-Morse A and B units were offered in road names that included the Chicago & North Western, Western Pacific, Wabash, Southern Pacific and Illinois Central. Locomotives included a 2-8-0 Consolidation, with the motor in the tender, and a little 0-4-0 dockside switcher.

1958

The Lionel-Rivarossi line sold well but Rivarossi could not keep up with the demand. Lionel did not know it, but they were too late

getting into the HO field and they were not going to catch up. Lionel was beset with internal problems. Sales had dropped from $22 million in 1956 to $18.7 million in 1957 and Joshua Cowen had retired. His son, Lawrence, was running the company, but Lawrence wanted to get out, too.

In the midst of this confusion, Lionel decided to expand their HO line in 1958, but they also decided to lower the quality — a major mistake in the quality-conscious HO field, which attracted many modelers. Lionel contracted with Athearn, an American manufacturer, to make the HO locos and add to the existing Rivarossi rolling stock.

An F-3 diesel was offered in road names that included the Denver & Rio Grande, Milwaukee Road, Baltimore & Ohio and New Haven. Also new was a Virginian rectifier that looked just like the O gauge model and a GP-7 in the Milwaukee Road and Wabash colors. The rectifier was also made in Pennsylvania and New Haven road names.

0581 Pennsylvania rectifier.

All these locos looked fine, but the motor that ran them was terrible. It had a rubber-band drive and constantly broke down.

A little Navy switcher and a Denver & Rio Grande snowplow were also offered.

The boxcars that Rivarossi introduced the year before were still available. New rolling stock made by Athearn in 1958 included a flat car with an airplane, a flat car with a boat, a crane car, and some New Haven passenger cars.

In 1959 Lionel decided to pour even more money into their HO line, even though in 1958 company sales dropped to $14.4 million and, for the first time since the Depression, Lionel registered a net loss — almost a half-million dollars. Management, in a state of chaos, made its uninspired decision to manufacture an HO line. It would require expensive new tooling but the confused company officers plunged forward anyway. They acquired Hobbyline, a small HO manufacturer, and used their dies for the new yard engine and the new freight cars.

The locomotives that Lionel made in 1959 included the Santa Fe, Texas Special and Alaskan Alcos, in ABA units; some yard switchers; a 4-6-2 Pacific; a Minneapolis & St. Louis rotary snowplow; and a gang car. None of them were particularly good runners.

0561 Rotary snowplow.

Lionel-made rolling stock predominated the line: boxcars, hoppers, cattle and poultry cars, a tank car and a circus car.

There were still some Athearn items for sale, but about all that was left of the Riverossi items were a derrick car and the Timken boxcar.

1960-1966

During this period Lionel made most of their own cars and they reflected the military and space trend of the hard-pressed O gauge line. Between 1959, when Roy Cohn took over operational control of Lionel, and 1963, when he got out, the company lost $14 million and Lionel was diversifying in so many directions little attention was being paid to the train end

of the business. While this did little good for O gauge sales, it was absolutely a disaster for the HO line. The HO customer's main interest was in scale size and authentic detail. Gimmick cars that had no basis in fact, shot rockets, or exploded when hit by a missile appalled the HO enthusiast.

"How would you like a car to explode on a trestle bridge, handmade out of toothpicks, that it took you four years to build?" asks one collector.

0850 Wood mock-up.

0850 Production model.

So, by the end of 1966, Lionel management had enough and left the HO market without ever having seriously entered it.

RATING

Lionel made a lot of HO, but it is hard to find anybody who actually collects it. It is the last of the untouched areas of Lionel collecting. It is still possible to find Lionel HO new in the box on hobby store shelves, where the stuff has sat since 1965 because HO modelers scoffed at it when it came out.

Perhaps HO will become more popular with collectors, not because of quality but because of availability, as other supplies dry up. But then again, perhaps HO will never catch on with collectors, since the O gauge market became looser when General Mills increased production. By 1978, Fundimensions was making models of such classics as the GG-1, the Virginia Rectifier, and the Budd cars, which led to a general lowering of prices for those same items built by Lionel in the 1940s and 1950s.

In any case, for those who are interested in HO, there were a total of 40 items made for Lionel by Rivarossi. All of them are the best and most desirable of Lionel's HO. These included eight boxcars in various road names, all of which were also used in O gauge.

Besides the boxcars, Rivarossi made a model of a Fairbanks-Morse C-liner diesel. It came in ABA units in six different road names — for a total of 18 different pieces. The road names were Western Pacific, Chicago & North Western, Wabash, Southern Pacific, and Illinois Central. No pecking order has been established as to which C-liners are more valuable than others, because, since there has been so little collector activity in this area, a pattern has yet to emerge.

Rivarossi also made two steamers — a 2-8-0 Consolidation, and an 0-4-0 docksider.

After the Rivarossi items, the next group in value are the Lionel HO made by Athearn. Within this Athearn group the most valued items at present are the three rectifiers — the Pennsylvania, the New Haven, and the Virginian. Next sought-after of the Athearn products are the geeps — the Northern Pacific, Wabash, and Milwaukee Road. After that comes the F-7 units — Milwaukee Road, Rio Grande, Baltimore & Ohio and New Haven.

The Minneapolis & St. Louis rotary snowplow is the hardest to find of the little Athearn yard locos.

Athearn also made some passenger sets, which came in three road names: Texas Special, Santa Fe, and Pennsylvania. The Pennsy was offered in maroon with a black roof. Later Lionel made all the same passenger cars, but this time the Pennsy cars were silver with a maroon roof.

Therefore, the hardest to find of all the passenger cars are the Athearn-built maroon Pennsylvanias. Next in value is the silver Pennsylvania with the maroon roof. All the rest of the passenger cars, either Athearn or Lionel-built, are about equal in availability.

All other Lionel-built HO items are more common and less desirable than the passenger cars, the other Athearn pieces, or the Rivarossi items.

MISCELLANEOUS

PAPER TRAIN

Lionel made a paper train in 1943, when World War II had caused a halt in the production of metal trains. The train had flanged wheels that rolled on a paper track by means of

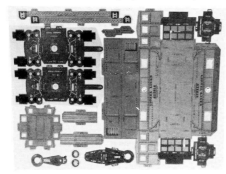

Paper train caboose 47618.

wooden axles. It came in a set which included three paper workmen, a crossing gate, a crossing signal, three crates and more than 16 feet of track, all made of paper.

The rolling stock included the 224 loco with 2224 tender (which closely resembled its prewar metal counterpart); 2812 red gondola; 61100 yellow automobile car; and 47618 red caboose.

Paper train tender 2224.

The three freight cars had "BLT 3-43" written on the side.

The Paper Train is very difficult to assemble.

Set number 50. Paper train box top.

LIONEL - AMERICAN FLYER

The year 1926 was the last that Lionel produced its 10 series freight cars, which had been replaced on the top-of-the-line by the new 200 series. But Lionel found another use for the 10 series in 1926. Some of the cars were supplied to American Flyer, which had just gone into the production of Standard gauge the year before and was not yet making its own freight cars.

The cars Lionel supplied Flyer had "American Flyer" stamped on the bottom and were

outfitted with riveted black American Flyer trucks. Thus, Lionel's number 12 gondola became the American Flyer 4007; Lionel's 13 stock car became Flyer's 4005; Lionel's 14 boxcar became Flyer's 4008; and Lionel's 17 caboose became Flyer's 4011.

These Lionel-Flyer cars were made only one year. In 1927 Flyer brought out its own line of freight cars, which, incidentally, many people felt were better looking than the boxier Lionel cars.

LIONEL - IVES

For several years after the bankruptcy of the Ives Corporation (covered in detail in Volume II), Lionel equipment appeared under the Ives name. The first year Lionel pieces showed up was 1929, the year after the bankruptcy, when the Lionel 8 electric was modified to the Ives 3236, the Lionel 248 was modified to the Ives 3260, and the Lionel 200 series tanker was placed on an American Flyer chassis and affixed with Ives trucks. That meant that the 1929 version of the Ives tanker was a hybrid of all three manufacturers. Also in 1929, the new operating pantographs from Lionel's 408E and 381E were used on the legendary Ives 3245.

Ives 3245R with Lionel pantographs.

By 1930 Lionel bodies made up a large portion of the items offered in the Ives catalog. These included both passenger and freight cars.

The Lionel 418, 419, 431, 490 large passenger cars were supplied to Ives, with Ives painting them in many different colors. Ives numbered the cars 246, 247, 248 and 249. These cars were supplied with Ives trucks and had the Lionel oil sticker removed from the bottom.

These passenger cars were offered in three different Ives sets: the *Chief*, in black and red, with either three or four cars; the *National Limited*, in blue and red in a four-car set; and the *Olympian*, in orange and black, with either three or four cars. In these sets, Ives supplied its own engines, either the 1134 steamer or the 3245 electric. They also placed the Ives six-wheel trucks on the cars, and the resulting sets are among the best looking Standard gauge sets made by anybody.

Ives also placed their own trucks on the freight cars Lionel supplied in 1930. The cars were from Lionel's 200 series. The following chart shows which Lionel cars became Ives.

Lionel Number	Ives Number	Ives Color
211 Flat	196	Light Green
212 Gondola	198	Black
213 Stock	193	Orange and Red
214 Box	192	Yellow and Peacock
215 Tank	190	Yellow and Red
217 Caboose	195	Maroon
219 Car	199	Dark Green and Peacock

Ives 249 observation using Lionel's 490 body (1930).

Ives 195 caboose using Lionel's 217 caboose body (1930).

In 1931 and 1932, with Lionel now in complete control of Ives, Lionel supplied the Bridgeport firm with regular Lionel stock items, which had Lionel trucks, couplers and colors. The cars were lettered "Ives Railway." The following are the numbers of items Lionel supplied to Ives in 1931 and 1932 and their corresponding Ives numbers:

Ives 1764 made by Lionel for Ives in 1932.

Lionel	Ives
10E	10E
390E	1770E
384E	1760E
511	1771
512	1772
513	1773
514	1774
516	1776
517	1777
514R	1778
332	332
339	339
341	341

Ives in 1932 came out with its 1764 electric and 1767, 1766 and 1768 passenger cars. All these were produced by Lionel and later the passenger cars became the transitional Lionel cars.

Also in 1931, Lionel supplied Ives with apple green 418s, 419s, 431s and 490s — all decaled with "Ives Railway."

COUPLERS

Short-straight hook
1906-1912

Long-straight hook
1906-1914

Short crinkle
1910-1916

Long crinkle
1910-1918

Hook with "ears"
1914-1926

Combination latch
1923-1928

Latch coupler
1924-1940

INVENTORY LIST

The years listed, are the years the items were cataloged. If an item was cataloged some years, then sold as an uncataloged item in other years, only the cataloged years are listed.

If an item was never cataloged, it is indicated by an asterisk (*). See text for colors and other information.

ACCESSORIES

025 Illuminated bumper 40-42
35 Boulevard lamp 40-42
43 Speedcraft 35, 36, 39-41
44 Speedcraft 35, 36
45N Auto. gateman 35, 36
46 Auto. crossing gate 39-42
47 Auto. double arm crossing gate 37-42
48W Station w/whistle 37-42
49 Airport 36-39
50 Electric airplane 36-39
52 Lamp post 33-41
53 Lamp post 31-42
54 Double bulb lamp post 29-35
55 Electric airplane set 36-39
56 Lamp post 24-42
57 Lamp post 24-42
58 Lamp post 24-42
59 Lamp post 24-36
060 Telegraph post 29-42
61 Lamp post 24-32, 34-36
62 Semaphore 24-32
63 Double bulb lamp post 33-42
64 Street lamp 40-42
65 Electric semaphore 24-36
66 Electric semaphore 24-36
67 Lamp post 24-32
068 Warning signal 25-42
069 Electric warning signal 24-35
69N Electric warning signal 36-39
071 Set of 6 060 posts
076 Block signal 24-28
76 Shack w/bell 39-42
077 Auto. crossing gate 24-35
77N Auto. crossing gate 36-39
078 Auto. train control 24-32
79 Flashing railroad signal 28-40
080 Electric semaphore 26-35
80N Auto. semaphore 36-42
082 Semaphore 28-35
82N Auto. semaphore 36-42
83 Traffic control signal 27-42
084 Hand controlled semaphore 27-32
85 Telegraph post 29-38, 40-42
87 Railroad crossing signal 27-42
89 Flag staff 23-34
90 Flag staff 27-42
91 Circuit breaker 29-42
092 Signal tower 24 27
93 Water tower 31-42
94 High tension tower 32-42
96 Coal elevator w/ hand crank 38-40

97 Electric coal elevator 38-42
98 Elevated coal storage bunker 39, 40
099 Train control 32-35
99N Auto. color light control bridge 36-42
105 Bridge approaches 24-31
106 3 section bridge 24-31
108 4 section bridge 24-31
109 5 section bridge 24-31
110 Bridge 24-31
112 Illuminated station 31-35
113 Illuminated station 31-34
114 Illuminated station 31-34
115 Illuminated station 35-42 (auto. start & stop)
116 Illuminated station 35-42 (auto. start & stop)
117 Illuminated station 36-42 (auto. start & stop, no outside lights)
121 Station 24-26
122 Illuminated station 24-30 (no corner platform lights)
124 Illuminated station 24-30, 33-36
125 Station, no lights 24, 25
126 Same as 125 but w/ lights 24-36
127 Illuminated station 24-36
128 Illuminated station w/ terrace 28-42
129 Terrace only 28-42
130 Curved tunnel 28
134 Illuminated station 37-42
136 Illuminated station 37-42
152 Auto. crossing gate 40-42
153 Auto. block signal 40-42
154 Auto. highway signal 40-42
155 Illuminated freight shed 31-42
156 Illuminated station platform 39-42
157 Hand truck 30-32
158 Station platform set 40-42
161 Baggage truck 30-32
162 Operating dump truck 30-32
163 Freight station set 30-32, 35-42
165 Triple action magnetic crane 40-42
184 Illuminated bungalow 24-32
185 Non-illuminated bungalow
186 Log loading outfit 40, 41
188 Coal elevator outfit 40, 41
189 Illuminated villa 24-31
191 Non-illuminated villa 24-32
205 Merchandise containers 31

206 Bag of scale coal 38-42
207 Bag of coal 39-42
208 Set of tools and chest 33-42
209 Set of 4 2 ¼" high barrels 33-42
0209 Set of 6 1 ½" barrels 33-42
270 Bridge w/ walkway 31-42
271 Two span bridge 31-33, 35-40
272 Three span bridge 31-33, 35-40
300 Hellgate bridge 28-42
308 Set of scale signs 40-42
313 Bascule bridge 40-42
314 Scale girder bridge 40-42
315 Illuminated trestle bridge 40-42
435 Power station 26-38
436 Power station 26-37
437 Power station with knife switches 26-37
438 Illuminated signal tower 27-40
439 Panel board w/ knife switches 28-42
0440 Position light signal bridge 32-35
440N Position light bridge
442 Landscape diner 38-42
444 Round house 32-34
550 Miniature figures set 32-36
551 Miniature engineer 32
552 Miniature conductor 32
553 Miniature porter w/ foot stool 32
554 Miniature male passenger 32
555 Miniature female passenger 32
556 Miniature red cap w/ luggage 32
840 Large power station 28-42
910 Grove of trees 32-42
911 Illuminated landscaped estate 32-42
912 Illuminated landscaped home 32-42
913 Illuminated landscaped bungalow 32-42
914 Park landscape 32-36
917 Valley & hills scenery 32
919 Bag of grass 32-36
922 Illuminated lamp terrace 32-36
927 Flag plot 37-42
1025 Illuminated bumper 40-42
1045 Crossing watchman 38-42
1560 Station for clockwork trains 34-37
1569 Accessory set for clockwork trains 34-37

LIONEL
Standard Gauge
Price and Rarity Guide
Also OO Gauge and 2 7/8-Inch Gauge

About This Guide

One Price

As with our other price and rarity guides, we list only one price. For items made in and after 1924, the grading standard we use is *Excellent.* We feel this is a reasonable standard for collectors to aspire to in acquiring items of this period. The chart at right tells how much to add or subtract to items found in better or worse condition than *Excellent.*

For items made before 1924 (the Early Period in our Table of Contents), our one price is based on items in *Very Good* condition, as defined by the standards of the Train Collectors Association and the Toy Train Operating Society. We chose *Very Good* because it is not realistic to expect a collector to assemble an Early Period collection whose average condition is better than *Very Good.* Use the TM Price Chart for calculating how much to subtract from the price of an item that is in less than *Very Good* condition, and how much to add to an item — for those few people who will ever find one — which is in better than *Very Good* condition.

TCA and TTOS Grading Standards

Mint	Brand new, unmarred, all original and unused.
Like New	Free of any blemishes, nicks, or scratches; original condition throughout, little sign of use.
Excellent	Minute nicks or scratches. No dents or rust.
Very Good	Few scratches, exceptionally clean; no dents.
Good	Scratches, small dents, dirty.
Fair	Well-scratched, chipped, dented, rusted or warped.
Poor	Beat-up, junk condition, some useable parts.

TM Price Chart

Condition	Add to or subtract from listed price
Mint Boxed	+ 40%
Mint (without box)	+ 30%
Like New	+ 10%
Excellent	Price Listed (1924 and after)
Very Good	Price Listed (before 1924)
Good	– 20%
Fair	– 30%
Poor	– 50% or more

Determining Prices

We send a list of items to prewar experts across the country. They assign a price and rarity rating to each item. Concurrently, the authors observe prices at train meets and prices advertised in the newsletters of collecting organizations. The prices and rarity ratings listed in this book are a consensus of this information.

Still, determining prices is a fallible undertaking. The sale price of an item will always be subject to several variables, including how eager the buyer is to buy and the seller to sell, the region of the country where the sale is made, the determination of condition by the parties involved, and the law of supply and demand. Under certain conditions, then, a price in this book may appear high or low to one side or the other in a deal. We are not the final authority. We show the way, not demand it. That's why we call this a price *Guide,* not a price *Mandate.*

Determining Rarity

We also ask our experts to indicate how rare an item is. Although it is often true that the rarer an item, the higher the price, it is by no means an inflexible truth. There are items that turn up with regularity but are in such great demand that they cost dearly. Conversely, some items are hard to find but have a low price tag because collectors are not that interested in them. Still we believe it is important for collectors to know how rare or common an item is no matter what its current value.

The system goes from 1, the most common with little or no collector interest, through 5, the rarest. To have a great collection, one should have some of the items that carry a rarity rating of 5 and most of those that carry a rating of 4.

No price is listed for **5+** or **5P** items because when so few items exist, sometimes only one, it is impossible to get a consensus. When a price is listed that was arrived at through the analysis of only a few sales (because only a few transpired), an * appears after the price. If an * appears without a price, it indicates no sales were reported. The following is our code to rarity:

5P   Prototypes of which there were one or two made.
Example: *Brass 0-6-0 O gauge prototype.*

5+   Pre-production mock-ups, factory mistakes, paint samples, or special items.
Example: *408E in dark green crackle.*

5   Extremely desirable, an item that is high-priced and in great demand. Usually difficult to find, but sometimes, just very expensive.
Examples: *Department Store Specials, 517 caboose with black roof, nickel-trimmed Blue Comet.*

4   Very collectible and hard-to-find, but likely to turn up at a large meet. Desirable. Examples: *440 Signal tower in aluminum and red, 116 Double-window station in green and cream.*

3   Somewhat hard-to-find and mildly desirable. Likely to turn up at large or medium-sized meets. Examples: *390E with black stripe, 514R Refrigerator car in ivory and peacock.*

2   Items that sold well and were available for a long time. Usually cataloged in low-priced sets and easy-to-find. Not much collector interest. Low priced. Examples: *517 Caboose in pea green with brass trim, 339 Series passenger cars in gray and maroon.*

1   Very little collector interest. Made in huge numbers. Common. Low priced. Examples: *Mojave 10E, 511 Flatcar in dark green.*

Variations

In most cases, we list only major variations. Major variations are worth more than normal versions. Minor variations – which are worth no more than normal versions – are not listed

Major variations come from normal production runs, can be readily seen, exist in sufficient numbers to be obtainable, and are accepted as collectible variations by the majority of experienced collectors. Examples would be a Hellgate bridge in the red, silver, and cream late colors, the nickel-trimmed Standard gauge Blue Comet, and the 514R Refrigerator car in white and light blue. These are major collectible variations and are important to collectors. They are included in this book.

Examples of minor variations would be slight differences in color, placement of the brakewheel on the right or left, presence or absence of an oil sticker, types of oil stickers, and types of journals. Changes were frequent in the Prewar era, often for no other reason than to use left-over inventories. For example, if, after copper journals were switched to nickel, a box of copper journals were found, they were used.

Making note of these minor variations in a price guide serves only to confuse the reader, clutter the guide, and make essential information harder to find.

Variations not listed are worth no more than the common or normal version. For example, the 184 and 185 villas are known to exist in at least twenty-four color variations. Most are worth about the same. We list six.

How To Use This Guide

The front of the book contains things of interest to most collectors – those items most likely to be traded. The items least likely to be traded are in the back. The first chapter contains accessories. Most prewar accessories can be used with both O gauge and Standard gauge, so collectors of both gauges will be interested in the accessory chapter. Some trackside accessories have two numbers – "O" preceding the number designates, not surprisingly, O Gauge. "N" after the number designates Standard gauge.

The most active and volatile Standard gauge era, the Classic Period, follows Accessories.

We placed the Early Period in the back of the book because there is less collector interest. Since so few items in the Early Period are actually traded, prices were determined by a much smaller sampling than the sampling used to determine prices in the Classic Period.

Items are listed by category in numerical order. Information is listed as follows: catalog number, type of item, years in the consumer catalog, rarity rating and price. The number in parenthesis is the rarity rating. The number on the extreme right in bold face is the average asking price in *Excellent* condition without the box.

Colors

The purpose of listing colors is to identify the item, not describe it in detail. For example, the 115 station is listed as cream and red. The base color and color of the window inserts and other trim are not listed because they don't affect price and they are not needed to identify the item.

The dominant color – usually the color of the body of cars and the walls of buildings – is listed first, followed by the color of the roof (if different), frame (if other than black), and the type or color of the trim.

In most cases, we use the color names established by the TCA in their book on prewar Lionel and we refer the reader to that excellent book for additional information on color and color variations.

In general, Lionel used dull colors (maroon, gray, and mojave) up to 1924, and bright colors (orange, cream, and green) with brass trim from 1924 to 1936. Standard gauge items made during the final years were painted cream, red, and silver.

Trim

Trim refers to the handrails, journals, number plates, brakewheels, window inserts, and other small items that were added to the item. Brass plates were used until 1935, when both brass plates and nickel plates were used. By 1938, only nickel plates were used. Nickel journals were used until 1929 or 1930, when they were changed to copper. Copper journals were used until 1934 or 1935, when they were changed back to nickel.

Although there are exceptions, nickel-trimmed items are more difficult to find and are worth more.

Warning

Trim can easily be switched. So can trucks, couplers, roofs, door guides, and bases of accessories.

It is highly unlikely a major variation is going to turn up in the 1990s, a variation that has gone undetected by thousands of collectors for more than 50 years. Have a healthy skepticism about unusual color schemes and odd combinations of trim.

Many fine reproductions and repaints have been made of the more desirable locos and cars. Some are not identified as reproductions. If you have doubt, seek the advice of an experienced collector.

If something sounds too good to be true, it probably isn't true.

Notice to Non-Collectors

A non-collector most often is selling a group of items at once and that lowers the price. Rare indeed is the non-collector who would lug the items to and from train meets, over a span of months, to sell them one at a time.

The non-collector's main concern should be with getting a fair price. A fair selling price for a non-collector may be arrived at by deducting 30% to 40% (depending on condition) from the price listed.

Trend Arrows ▲ ▼

Trend Arrows indicate growth or decline in demand. If there is no discernible trend, no arrow will appear.

Is Standard Gauge Dead?

"Not Classic Period Lionel," says Frank Petruzzo, in emphatic opposition to the generally accepted belief. Frank is a knowledgeable Standard Gauge collector and possessor of probably the top Lionel Classic Period collection in the world (his collection includes eleven different State Sets and eleven different Blue Comet sets). "Classic Period Lionel has never been hotter and prices have never been higher," says Frank. "The demand for *Excellent* or better is strong and getting stronger."

Frank also does not agree with those who say everyone collects the toys they had as kids. "The average age of a knowledgeable Standard gauge collector is 45 to 50," says Frank. "They are guys who never had much Standard gauge as a kid but who have developed sophisticated tastes over the years and who appreciate the fine train art of the Classic Period."

Frank believes a true collector goes beyond what he was familiar with in his youth. "He probably starts with what he had as a kid but a true collector keeps learning. Guys who aren't open to expanding their horizons are accumulators – not collectors. A true collector borders on being obsessive. He truly loves his trains, learns all about them, is constantly researching and is constantly trying to upgrade. He admires his trains, cherishes them like an art collector might cherish a Van Gogh or a Renoir or a Picasso."

Frank recently paid at auction $11,900 (plus the 10% buyer's premium) for a *Like New,* boxed 9U with three 418 series cars in orange. The set was made for a department store in Pittsburgh and came in a box with the uncataloged number *PO 50.* "I wanted this set because of the box. It is an extremely rare uncataloged set even though the contents were cataloged."

Did Frank pay too much? "I guess the other guys bidding against me thought I did because they dropped out. But I don't think so. I feel the orange 9 sets have been undervalued. They are much rarer than State Sets. I'd buy another just like this for the same price."

Frank visualizes the day in the not-too-distant future when the top Standard gauge collectors in the world meet in Europe for a special auction. "Classic Period Standard gauge comes closer to being art than any other era. The demand for *Ex* and *LN* is getting stronger and those who collect it are getting more aggressive and are willing to pay almost any price. I can see the day when major collectors convene in Paris, where auctions for the great masters of the art world are held, and have a special auction of top Classic Period Standard gauge. Unheard of prices will be paid because Standard gauge is art and can only be appreciated by a true collector who has a collector's heart. If you have to ask what that means, you are no collector. You are an accumulator."

Abbreviations

alum	Aluminum
blk	Black
bj	Black journals
bnt org	Burnt orange
brn	Brown
crm	Cream
dk	Dark
D-C	Distant Control
DSS	Department Store Special
E	Automatic reverse unit
FAOS	F.A.O. Schwarz
grn	Green
HS	Heat-stamped
IC	Illinois Central
LH	Left-hand switch
LL	Lionel Lines
litho	Lithographed
lt	Light
mar	Maroon
N-D	Non-derailing switch
nj	Nickel journals
NYC	New York Central
NYC & HRRR	New York Central & Hudson River RR
NDV	No difference in value
NYNH&H	New York, New Haven & Hartford
ob	Original box
Obvs	Observation
org	Orange
PRR	Pennsylvania Railroad
RH	Right-hand switch
rd	Red
RS	Rubber-stamped
SG grn	Stephen Girard green
T&W	Indicates tender comes with whistle
U	Uncataloged
W	Whistle
wht	White
X	Indicates different from normal production – higher couplers, different trim, color, etc.
yell	Yellow
4W	Four-wheel trucks
6W	Six-wheel trucks

Contents

Accessories
Stations

48W	Whistling Station lithograph 37-42	(1)	25

Single Window Stations 31-42
1. Cream/green

112	No outside lights 31-35	(3)	300
113	Outside lights 31-34	(4)	325

2. Ivory/red

115	Outside lights 36-42 *Automatic Train Control*	(4)	350
117	No outside lights 36-42 *Automatic Train Control*	(3)	300

Double Window Stations 31-42
1. Cream/green

114	No *Automatic Train Control* 31-34	(4)	1500
116	*Automatic Train Control* 35,36	(4)	1800

2. Ivory/red

116	*Automatic Train Control* 36-42	(4)	1600

Lionel City Stations 1920-36
Note: Lionel City Stations come with or without departure board. NDV

121	**No lights 20-26** Salmon/pea green 20-26	(3)	200
122	**Interior light 20-31**		
	1. Salmon/pea green	(3)	200
	2. Terra cotta/pea green		
123	**Interior light 20-23** Salmon/pea green 20-23	(3)	200
124	**Interior light plus two exterior corner lights** 1920-30, 1933-36		
	1. Brown/pea green	(3)	200
	2. Burnt orange/pea green	(3)	200
	3. Salmon/pea green	(3)	200
	4. Terra cotta/pea green	(3)	200
	5. Tan/red	(4)	300
134	**124 Tan/red 37-42** With *Automatic Train Control*	(4)	300

Lionelville Stations 23-42
Note: Numerous color variations exist. NDV

125	**Brick lithograph/pea green 23-25** No lights	(3)	125
126	**23-36 Inside light**		
	1. Crackle red/maroon/mojave	(3)	125
	2. Crackle red/pea green/mojave	(3)	125
	3. Brick litho/pea green/flat light gray	(3)	125
	4. Mustard/light red/green	(4)	165
136	**37-42 Interior light *Automatic Train Control***		
	1. Mustard/red/green	(4)	150
	2. Cream/red/green	(3)	125
	3. Yellow/red/green	(3)	125

Lioneltown Stations
Note: Numerous color variations exist. NDV

127	**23-36 Interior light**		
	1. Ivory/red/mojave	(2)	75
	2. White/light red/mojave	(3)	100
	3. White/light red/mustard	(3)	100
	4. Mustard/maroon/gray	(3)	100
137	**37-42 Interior light *Automatic Train Control***		
	1. White/red/mustard	(3)	100
	2. White/red/light mojave	(3)	100

Platform & Terrace Stations

128	**Lionel City Station & Terrace Platform 28-42** 129 Platform in combination with:		
	1. Lionel City Stations 28-30 Stations 121, 122 & 124	(4)	1500
	2. Single Window Stations 31-36 Stations 112 & 113	(4)	1500
	3. 115 Single Window Station 37-42	(5)	1500
129	**Terrace Station Platform 28-33,35-42**		
	1. Light mojave/pea grn lattice 28-33 gold light posts	(4)	900
	2. Cream/cream 35-42 aluminum light posts	(5)	2000
131	**Corner Display Platform 24-28** Part of set 198	(4)	275
132	**Corner Display Platform 24-28** Part of set 198	(4)	275
133	**Heart Shaped Display Platform 24-28** Part of set 198	(4)	275
134	**Oval Shaped Display Platform 24-28** Part of set 198	(4)	275
135	**Circular Platform 24-28** Part of set 199	(4)	275
136	**Large Elevation 24-28** Part of set 199	(4)	
155	**Freight Shed 30-42 illuminated**		
	1. Terra cotta/maroon 30-42	(3)	400
	2. Red/gray 40-42	(4)	450
156	**Illuminated Station Platform 39-42**		
	1. Grn base/vermilion roof/silver posts	(3)	100
	2. Grn base/vermilion roof/gray posts	(4)	150
158	**Station Platform Set 40-42** Two 156 Station Platforms and one 136 Station in set box	(4)	300
198	**Large Platform Set 24-28**	(4)	1750
199	**Small Platform Set 24-28**	(4)	
435	**Power Station 26-38**		
	1. Mustard/mojave/gray	(3)	200
	2. Cream/terra cotta/gray	(4)	250
	3. Mustard/terra cotta/gray	(3)	200
	4. Cream/light mojave/green	(4)	250

436	**Power Station 26-37**		
	1. Terra cotta/mustard	(3)	200
	2. Same as 1 with *Edison Service* sign over door rather than the common *Power Station*	(5)	650
	3. Cream/terra cotta	(3)	200
	4. Cream/light mojave	(4)	300
840	**Power Station 28-42**		
	1. Cream/orange/mojave floor 28-34	(4)	2200
	2. Cream/orange/gray floor 35-42	(5)	3000
1560	**Station 33-37 Lithograph Clockwork Sets**		
	1. Terra cotta base	(3)	25
	2. Dark green base	(4)	25

Towers and Railroad Structures

092	**Signal Tower 23-28**		
	1. White/red/mojave	(3)	75
	2. Terra cotta/red/mojave	(4)	90
	3. Light terra cotta/pea green/ivory	(3)	75
	4. Terra cotta/pea green/mustard	(3)	75
92	**Floodlight Tower 31-42**		
	1. Orange base/pea grn tower 31-34	(3)	150
	2. Red base/aluminum tower 35-40	(2)	125
	3. Red base/gray tower 40-42	(4)	250
93	**Water Tower 31-42 and postwar**		
	1. Terra cotta/pea green tank	(3)	45
	2. Aluminum/aluminum tank /decal	(2)	35
	3. Gray/aluminum tank/decal	(4)	100
	4. Gray/gray tank/decal	(5)	150
94	**High Tension Tower 32-42**		
	1. Terra cotta base, dark gray tower 32-34	(4)	300▲
	2. Red/aluminum tower 35-40	(3)	300
	3. Red/gray tower 41,42	(5)	500▲
200	**Turntable 28-36 manual**		
	1. Pea green/red center/brass	(3)	250▼
	2. Black/red center/brass	(4)	600 ▼
437	**Switch Signal Tower 26-37**		
	1. Burnt orange/mustard/peacock roof	(3)	350▼
	2. Terra cotta/cream/pea green roof	(4)	450
	3. Cream/orange roof	(5)	3500▲
438	**Signal Tower 27-39**		
	1. Orange/red/pea green, no switches 27	(4)	400
	2. Same with knife switches 28-35	(3)	275▼
	3. Orange/maroon/pea green	(3)	275▼
	4. White/red/silver 36-39	(3)	450
439	**Panel Board 28-42**		
	1. Crackle maroon/white	(3)	150
	2. Maroon/black panel	(3)	125
	3. Red/black	(3)	125
	4. Aluminum/white	(4)	175
440	**Signal Bridge 32-35**		
0440	1. Gray/maroon/terra cotta 32-34	(2)	300▲
	2. Aluminum/red/red 35	(4)	400▲

440N Signal 36-42
1. Aluminum/red/red (2) 275
2. Gray/red/red (4) 350

441 Weighing Scale 27-40 with brass weights
Cream/crackle maroon/pea green (4) 1000▲

442 Landscaped Diner 38-42 (3) 200
610 Ivory/red passenger car on wood base

444 Roundhouse Section 32-34 (5) 3500
Terra cotta/pea green

Operating Accessories

96 Manual Coal Elevator 38-40 (4) 150
Aluminum/yellow/red roof

97 Remote Control Coal Elevator 38-42
1. Aluminum/yellow/red roof (2) 125
2. Gray/yellow/red roof (4) 175

98 Elevated Coal Storage Bunker 39,40 (4) 250▲
Aluminum/yellow/red roof

164 Remote Control Log Loader 40-42
1. Green/cream/aluminum/light red (2) 200
2. Green/cream/92 gray/light red (4) 200

165 Magnetic Crane 40-42
1. Aluminum superstructure (3) 200
2. Gray superstructure (4) 250

313 *See Bridges*

Trackside Accessories

Note: "O" designates item made for O Gauge.
"N" designates Standard Gauge.

013 D-C Switch & Panel Board Set 29-31 (5) 150
012 (Pair) 439

27N Lighting Set for early cars 11-23 (4) 30

043 Bild-A-Motor Gear Set 29 (4)

45 Gateman 35,36 Green/ivory/vermilion roof
045 1. Blue gateman (2) 40
2. Brown gateman (5) 50

45N Gateman 37-42 (Same as 45/045)
1. Silver crossing post 37-40 (1) 40
2. Gray crossing post 41,42 (4) 60

46 Single Arm Crossing Gate 38-42
1. Green/aluminum gate (2) 75
2. Green/gray gate (4) 100

47 Double Arm Crossing Gate 38-42
1. Green/aluminum gate (2) 100
2. Green/92 gray gate (4) 125

60N Telegraph Post 20-35
1. Gray/gray/maroon (2) 35
2. Peacock/peacock/red (3) 40
3. Apple green/apple green/maroon (3) 30

060 Telegraph Post 29-42 O gauge
w/track extension arm
1. Orange/orange/maroon (2) 35
2. Peacock/peacock/red (3) 40
3. Gray/gray/light red (4) 45

62 Semaphore 20-32 single arm
1. Dark green/yellow (3) 30
2. Pea green/pea green (2) 25
3. Apple green/apple green (4) 40

63 Semaphore 15-20 single arm (4) 25
Black/orange/dark green

64 Semaphore 15-21 double arm (4) 40
Black/orange/dark green

65 Semaphore 15-26 single arm illuminated
Black/cream/orange
1. Notched arm (4) 40
2. Unnotched arm (5) 50

66 Semaphore 15-28 double arm (5) 45
Black/orange/dark green

68 Warning Signal 20-39 (1) 5
068 Warning Signal 25-42 (1) 5

69 Warning Bell 21-35
069 1. Maroon/brass/black (3) 50▲
2. Olive green/black/brass (2) 45▲

69N Warning Bell 36-42 (3) 40
Red or aluminum. NDV

70 Accessory Set 21-25 (5) 150
O & Standard gauge
1 59 Lamp Post, 2 62 Semaphores,
1 68 Warning Signal

71 Set of Six 60 Telegraph Poles w/box 21-31
1. Gray/gray/maroon (2) 200
2. Peacock/peacock/red (3) 250
3. Apple green/apple green/maroon (3) 200

071 Set of Six 060 TelegraphPoles w/box 29-42
1. Orange/orange/maroon (3) 225
2. Green/green/red (3) 250
3. Gray/gray/light red (4) 300

76 Block Signal 23-29 illuminated
076 1. Mojave (2) 100
2. White (3) 100

76 Watchman's Shack 39-42 (4) 200
with Ringing Bell, Red/white/orange

77 Crossing Gate 23-35
077 1. Black/black and white arm/unlighted (4) 60
2. Black/red and white/unlighted (3) 50
3. Dark gray/black and white/lighted (3) 50
4. Dark green/green and white/lighted (3) 50
5. Pea green/black and white/lighted (3) 50

77N Crossing Gate 36-39 (2) 40
Black/red lighted

78 Block Signal 24-32
078 1. Maroon base/mojave post (4) 150
2. Orange base/cream post (3) 100

79 Railroad Crossing Signal 28-40
1. Cream 28-34 (3) 75
2. Aluminum 36-40 (4) 100

80 Operating Semaphore 26-35
080 1. Black/mojave (3) 75
2. Terra cotta/mojave (4) 80

80N Operating Semaphore 36-42 (3) 100
Red/aluminum/orange

82 Operating Semaphore 27-35
082 1. Peacock/cream/number plate (4) 150
2. Peacock/cream/no number plate (4) 125
3. Green/aluminum/no number plate (3) 125

82N Operating Semaphore 36-42 (2) 125
Green/aluminum/black

83 Traffic Control Signal 27-42
1. Mojave/cream (4) 125
2. Red/cream (3) 100
3. Light red/cream/white (3) 100

84 Operating Semaphore 27-32 manual (4) 100
084 Dark green/cream/orange

85 Telegraph Post with extension arm 29-42
1. Orange/orange/maroon (2) 35
2. Aluminum/aluminum/red (4) 40
3. Gray/gray/red (4) 50

86 Set of Six 85 Telegraph Poles 29-42
1. Orange/orange/maroon (2) 300
2. Aluminum/aluminum/red (4) 350
3. Gray/gray/red (4) 350

87 Railroad Crossing Signal 27-42
1. Mojave/orange (4) 75
2. Dark green/pea green (5) 125
3. Dark green/cream (3) 100

097 Telegraph Post Set 34, 35 (3) 100
with 6 Pea green/pea green-red 096 poles
(sold only in this set) and 068 warning sign

99 Train Control Block Signal 32-35
099 1. Black/ivory/black (2) 75
2. Red/ivory/black (2) 75
3. Black/light mojave/red (2) 75

99N Train Control Block Signal 36-42 (2) 75
Red/aluminum/red

152 Crossing Gate 40-42 and postwar
1. Red base/aluminum gates (1) 25
2. Red base/gray gates (3) 40
3. Red base/white gates (5) 50

153 Block Signal 40-42 and postwar
1. Green/aluminum post/orange (1) 25
2. Green/gray post/orange (3) 50

154	Highway Crossing Signal 40-42 and postwar		
	1. Red or orange base/silver post 40	(5)	75
	2. Black/aluminum 40 and postwar	(1)	25
	3. Black/gray 41,42	(3)	35

163 Freight Station Set 30-42
2 157 Handtrucks, 1 161 Baggage Truck,
1 162 Dump Truck

	1. Large box illustrated display insert	(4)	200*
	2. Small box no insert	(3)	175*

193	Accessory Set 27-29	(5)	400*

1 each: 069 Warning Bell, 076 Block Signal,
077 Automatic Crossing Gate, 078 Automatic
Train Control Signal, 080 Semaphore

194	Box Set 27-29	(4)	500

Contains 1 each 69, 76, 77, 78, 80

196	Accessory Set 27	(5)	500*

O & Standard gauge
2 58 Lamp Posts, 6 60 Telegraph Poles,
62 Semaphore, 68 Warning Signal, 127 Station

1045 Operating Watchman 38-42, 46-50 (postwar carry-over)

	1. Black uniform	(4)	35
	2. Brown uniform	(3)	35
	3. Blue uniform/silver post	(1)	25
	4. Blue uniform/gray post	(3)	30

1569	Accessory Set 34-37	(4)	50

4 1571 Telegraph Poles, 1572 Semaphore,
1573 Warning Signal, 1574 Clock, 1575 Gate

Street Lamps and Lightposts

35 Boulevard Lamp 40-42 and postwar

	1. Aluminum	(2)	30
	2. 92 Gray	(3)	50

52	Street Lamp 33-41 aluminum	(3)	75

53 Street Lamp 31-42

	1. Light mojave	(3)	45
	2. Light ivory	(3)	45
	3. Aluminum	(4)	50

54 Small Double Gooseneck Lamp 29-35

	1. Pea green	(3)	40
	2. State brown	(5)	50
	3. Green	(4)	50
	4. Maroon	(5)	50

56 Park Lamp Post 24-42, 46-49 (postwar carry-over)

	1. Dark gray	(3)	35
	2. Gray	(3)	30
	3. Mojave	(3)	30
	4. Green	(1)	25
	5. Pea green	(2)	25
	6. Copper	(5)	50
	7. Aluminum	(5)	50

57 Broadway Lamp Post 22-42

	1. Gray	(3)	75
	2. Yellow	(4)	100
	3. Orange	(2)	75

Note: All three colors exist with the following celluloid printed lamp shades in either silver or black lettering. Silver lettering is harder to find:

a. Broadway & Main	(1)	
b. Broadway & 21st Street	(4)	
c. Fifth Avenue & 21st Street	(5)	
d. Fifth Avenue & 42nd Street	(4)	
e. Broadway & Fifth Avenue	(2)	
f. Broadway & 42nd Street	(2)	

58 Small Gooseneck Lamp 22-42, 46-50 (postwar carry-over)

	1. Maroon	(2)	30
	2. Green	(2)	30
	3. Pea Green	(3)	35
	4. Aluminum	(5)	40
	5. Cream	(1)	30

59 Gooseneck Lamp 20-36

	1. Dark green	(2)	35
	2. Olive green	(1)	30
	3. State brown	(5)	60
	4. Pea green	(2)	35
	5. Mojave	(5)	60
	6. Maroon	(5)	60
	7. Red	(5)	75

61 Large Gooseneck Lamp 14-32, 34-36

	1. Black	(5)	75
	2. Dark green	(3)	40
	3. Olive green	(3)	40
	4. Maroon	(2)	35
	5. Mojave	(4)	40

63	Twin Street Lamp 33-42	(4)	200

Aluminum

64	Highway Lamp 40-42 and postwar	(3)	50

Green

67 Large Twin Gooseneck 15-32

	1. Dark green/large shade	(5)	100
	2. Dark green/small shade	(3)	50
	3. State brown	(4)	75

111 Lamp Assortment 20-31

	1. Wooden lamp boxes	(5)	200
	2. Cardboard lamp boxes	(4)	100

Tunnels and Mountains

118	Tunnel 20-32 metal no light	(1)	35
118L	Tunnel 27 illuminated	(5)	50
119	Tunnel 20-42 no light	(1)	40
119L	Tunnel 27-33 illuminated	(5)	75
120	Tunnel 20-27	(3)	75
120L	Tunnel 27-42 illuminated	(1)	75
123	Tunnel 33-42 90 degree curve O gauge	(3)	100
130	Tunnel 24-26 90 degree curve O gauge	(5)	250
130L	Tunnel 27-33 Same as 130 but illuminated	(5)	325
140L	Tunnel 27-32 O or Standard gauge 90 degree curve	(4)	750
915	Tunnel 32-34 90 degree curve Standard gauge	(5)	750
915	Tunnel 1935 90 degree curve O gauge, slightly smaller than previous 915	(5)	275
916	Tunnel 1932 90 degree curve O gauge handpainted	(3)	150
916	Tunnel 33-42 90 degree curve Slightly smaller than previous 916	(2)	150
917	Mountain 32-36 O or Standard gauge Handpainted scenic hillside	(5)	300
918	Mountain 32-36 O or Standard gauge Handpainted scenic hillside	(5)	300
923	Tunnel 33-42 O or Standard gauge	(4)	200
924	Tunnel 35-42 072 gauge 90 degree turn	(4)	180
1022	Tunnel 35-42 Lionel Jr. and small O gauge 90 degree turn	(1)	25
1023	Tunnel 34-42 Handpainted/Lionel Jr. and small O gauge	(3)	25

Standard Gauge Bridges

104 Center Span & Approaches 20-31
Pea green/cream and olive green/cream. NDV

100	Two Approaches	(2)	40
101	Two Approaches, one Center Span	(2)	65
102	Two Approaches, two Center Spans	(2)	100
103	Two Approaches, three Center Spans	(2)	125
104	Center Span	(3)	25

280	Steel Girder Bridge 31-33	(3)	40

Red, pea green, olive green, green. NDV

280X	280 Bridge	(4)	35

modified to fit O gauge track

281	280 Bridge Span 31-33 set of 2	(4)	200
282	280 Bridge Span 31-33 set of 3	(4)	250

300 Hellgate 28-42 O or Standard gauge

	1. Pea green/cream/orange	(4)	1000
	2. Aluminum/ivory/red	(5)	1350

Scenic Plots

89	**Flag Pole** 23-34 Ivory	(2)	60
90	**Flag Staff and Flag** 27-42	(3)	100
184	**Bungalow** 23-32 lighted	(3)	50

185 **Bungalow** 23,24 unlighted
1. Ivory/dark green/gray	(5)	100▲
2. Flesh/orange/gray	(4)	60
3. Cream/red/gray	(4)	60
4. White/apple green/Hiawatha gray	(4)	50
5. Yellow/red/Hiawatha gray	(4)	50
6. Lithograph	(2)	40

186 **Bungalow Set** 23-32 Lighted
5 184 Bungalows
1. Large box illustrated display insert	(4)	400*
2. Small box no insert	(4)	350*

187 **Bungalow Set**
Five lithographed 185 bungalows	(4)	400▲

189 **Villa** 23-32
1. Ivory/dark gray/pea green	(4)	160
2. Ivory/maroon/pea green	(3)	140
3. Sand/peacock/terra cotta	(4)	160
4. Light mustard/apple green/ Hiawatha gray	(4)	160

191 **Villa** 23-32
1. Brick litho/ pea green/mojave	(4)	150
2. Terra cotta/pea green/mojave	(3)	120
3. Red crackle/pea green/mojave	(3)	120
4. Cream/red/Hiawatha gray	(4)	150

Note: 184,185,189, and 191 come in many different variations. For a complete list refer to the TCA's book on prewar Lionel.

192 **Villa and Bungalow Set** 23-32 (4) 600
Two 184, one 189 villa, and one 191 villa in assorted colors

195 **Illuminated Terrace** 27-30 (5) 750
Contains 90 flag, 184 bungalow, two 56 lamp posts, 189 villa, and 191 villa

910 **Grove of Trees** 32-42 (4) 250

911 **Illuminated Country Estate** 32-42
Wood base covered with shrubbery and trees around 191 villa/many variations. NDV
1. Terra cotta/pea green/mojave	(3)	300
2. Crackle red/pea green/mojave	(4)	400
3. Yellow/red/gray	(3)	400

912 **Illuminated Suburban Home** 32-42
Wood base covered with shrubbery and trees around 189 villa/many variations. NDV
1. Mojave/white/dark gray	(3)	325
2. Gray/ivory/apple green	(4)	350
3. Terra cotta/white/pea green	(3)	325
4. Ivory/cream/mojave	(5)	400
5. Light mustard/apple green/gray	(4)	400

913 **Illuminated Landscaped Bungalow** 32-42
Wood base covered with shrubbery and trees around 184 bungalow
1. Lithographed	(3)	275
2. Cream/red/mojave	(3)	275
3. Ivory/red/gray	(2)	250
4. Ivory/apple green/gray	(3)	275
5. Yellow/red/gray	(4)	300

914 **Park Landscape** 32-36 (3) 250
Wood base with trees, shrubbery, and garden base with flowers

920 **Illuminated Scenic Park** 32,33 (5) 2000
Two sections, two 189 villas, two 191 villas, and two 184 bungalows

921 **Illuminated Scenic Park** 32,33 (5) 3000
Three sections, two 920 end sections, and one 921C center section

921C **Illuminated Center Section** 32,33 (5) 1250
Contains one 189 villa, 191 villa, 184 bungalow, 910 grove of trees, 914 park landscape, or 922 illuminated lamp terrace.

922 **Lamp Terrace** 32-36 (5) 200
(56 lamp/copper)

927 **Ornamental Flag Plot** 37-42 (3) 250

Miscellaneous

2	**Figure Set** (seated) 10-18	(5)	300
125	**Track Template** 38	(5)	5

157 **Hand Truck** 30-32
1. Dark red	(2)	25
2. Red	(3)	30

161 **Baggage Truck** 30-32
1. Pea green RS *Lionel Lines*	(3)	50
2. Pea green no RS	(3)	50
3. Green no RS	(2)	50

162 **Dump Truck** 30-32
1. Yellow/green bin	(4)	60
2. Orange/blue bin	(3)	50
3. Orange/peacock bin	(2)	40

Note: Bins can be switched

205 **LCL Containers** 30-38 (set of three) (3) 300
Hinged doors, brass trim, dark green

208 **Tool Set** 34-42
1. Dark gray painted chest	(3)	75
2. Silver painted chest	(3)	75
Includes hoe, sledge hammer, pick, shovel, axe, and rake		
3. 92 gray	(4)	100

209	**Set of 4 Barrels** 30-42 Std. Gauge	(2)	15
0209	**Set of 6 Barrels** 30-42 O gauge	(2)	15
308	**Set of Yard Signs** 40-42 and postwar	(2)	25

550 **Set of Six Standing Figures** 32-36 (3) 225
In original box w/insert (4) 350

551	**Engineer** 32 (oil can spout usually broken off)		
	1. Powder blue	(3)	40
	2. Medium blue	(3)	40

552 **Conductor** 32
1. Navy uniform	(3)	30
2. Black uniform	(3)	30

553 **Porter** 32 Navy uniform (3) 40
With step box

554 **Male Passenger** 32
1. Brown overcoat	(3)	35
2. Gray overcoat	(3)	35

555 **Female Passenger** 32
1. Maroon overcoat	(3)	30
2. Brown overcoat	(3)	30
3. Green overcoat	(4)	35

556	**Red Cap** 32	(3)	40
812T	**Tool Set**	(3)	30
919	**Sack of Grass** 32-42	(1)	10
925	**Lubricant** 35-42	(1)	5

Paper Train 43,44 (4) 300
Note: Price based on complete set unassembled in box.

Non-Train Production

3 **Pleasure Boat** 33-36 (4) 400
White/vermilion/cream top - two figures in front - with display stand

44 **Racing Boat** 35,36 (5) 500
White/green/dark brown top two figures with display stand

49 **Airport** 37-39 58" diameter cardboard (5) 500
base/color lithograph

50 **Airplane** 36 with pylon and controls (3) 1000

51 **Airport** 36,38 (5) 500
Square cardboard airport/color lithograph

55 **Airplane** 37-39 (4) 1000
with pylon and controls

80 **Racing Car Set** 12-16 (5) 3000*
One orange or red car, two figures, 36" diameter track circle with starting post

81 Same as 80 with 30" diameter track circle

84 **Two Race Sets** 12-16 *

85 **Racing Car Set** *
one 80 and one 81 racing car

455 **Electric Range** 30, 32,33 (4) 1000

1500 **Locoscope** 39 (4) 150▲
Viewer in the shape of a steam locomotive with thirty-nine black & white pictures on 16mm film

Standard Gauge Classic Era
Electric Locomotives

8   0-4-0 25-32
8E
1. Maroon/brass	(2)	175
2. Olive green/brass	(2)	175
3. Mojave/brass	(3)	200
4. Red/cream stripe/cream trim	(2)	175
5. Red/no stripe/brass	(3)	200
6. Dark olive green/brass U	(5)	500
7. Maroon/cream stripe/cream trim U	(4)	350
8. Pea green/yellow U	(4)	350
9. Peacock/orange/orange stripe U	(5)	500
10. Peacock/cream stripe/cream trim U	(5)	500
11. Dark green/brass U	(4)	500

9   0-4-0 *NYC* 29 manual reverse   (5)   2800
Dark green

9E   0-4-0 *NYC* 28-30
1. Orange	(4)	1500
2. SG two-tone green	(4)	1750
3. Dark gray	(3)	1200

9U   0-4-0 *U-Build It* Kit Orange 28,29
Same as 9E but hand reverse
1. Unassembled in box complete	(5)	4000
2. Assembled no box	(4)	1800

10   0-4-0 *CM&St.P* 25-30
10E
1. Mojave	(1)	175
2. Gray	(2)	175
3. Peacock	(1)	175
4. Peacock/orange stripe	(3)	200
5. Peacock/dk green frame cream stripe U	(4)	400
6. Red/cream stripe U	(4)	400
7. Red/no cream stripe U	(4)	350
8. Tan U	(3)	500
9. Olive U	(3)	600
10. State brown/dk green frame cream U	(4)	600
11. Mojave/cream stripe	(3)	250

318   0-4-0 *NYC* 1924-35
318E
1. Dark gray	(2)	300
2. Mojave	(2)	300
3. Gray	(1)	250
4. Pea green	(1)	250
5. State brown/cream stripe	(4)	600
6. State brown/no cream stripe	(4)	600
7. Black (headed Coal Train)	(5)	2000

380   0-4-0 *CM&St.P* 23-29
380E
1. Mojave	(4)	700
2. Maroon	(2)	400
3. Dark greenw/weighted frame	(4)	550
4. Same w/o weighted frame	(3)	400

381   4-4-4 *CM&St.P* 28-36
381E
1. State green/apple green/381E	(4)	2500
2. State green/red/381E	(5)	3000

381U   4-4-4 *U-Build-It Kit* 28,29 (in box)
1. Kit in box	(5)	6500
2. Dark State green/381U plate	(5)	*
3. Dark State green/381 plate	(5)	3500

402   0-4-4-0 *NYC* 23-29 2 motors
402E
1. Mojave/strap headlight	(4)	600
2. Mojave/cast headlight	(3)	550

Note: Early 402s came with the E rubber-stamped on the door. These are rarer than those with the E on the brass plate. Add $50

408E   0-4-4-0 *NYC* 27-36 2 motors
1. Mojave	(3)	1000
2. Apple green	(2)	1200
3. Dark green (State Set)	(5)	3500
4. Tan (State Set)	(4)	3500
5. Tan/dark brown roof (State Set)	(5)	4000

Steam Locomotives

384   2-4-0 384T Black 30-32   (2)   500
384E   Came with or without green stripe and either brass or green window trim. NDV

385E   2-4-2 384T 385T 33-39
1. Gunmetal/copper and brass 384T 33	(4)	750
2. Gunmetal/nickel 384T, 34	(2)	650
3. Gunmetal/nickel Ives 385T 35-39	(5)	850

390   2-4-2 390T 1929 only
Black with or w/o orange stripe   (4)   850
hand rev

390E   2-4-2 390T 390X 29-31,33
1. Black/orange stripe	(3)	800
2. Blue/cream stripe *Blue Comet*	(4)	1500
3. Dk green/orange stripe dark green stripe	(4)	1700
4. Same as 3 with light green stripe	(5)	2000
5. Black/red stripe	(3)	1500

392E   4-4-2 384T 392T 32-39
1. Black/brass and copper/384T with or without green stripe. NDV	(3)	1200
2. Black/384T black crackle finish	(5)	2000
3. Black/brass and copper/12w 392T	(5)	2300
4. Black/nickel/12w 392T	(4)	1700
5. Gunmetal/nickel/12w 392T	(4)	1600

400E   4-4-4 400T 31-39
1. Blk/brass & copper brass boiler bands	(3)	2200
2. Blk/brass & copper/painted bands	(4)	2700
3. Gunmetal/brass & copper brass bands	(3)	2200
4. Gunmetal/br & copper painted bands	(4)	2500
5. Black crackle/brass	(5)	5000
6. Black crackle/nickel	(4)	3000
7. Blue/brass and copper	(4)	3000
8. Light blue/nickel	(4)	3500
9. Gunmetal/nickel painted boiler bands	(4)	3000
10. Black/nickel	(5)	2750

1835E   2-4-2 34-39 same as 385E
1. Black/nickel/384T 34	(3)	650
2. Black/nickel/1835TW 35-39	(4)	850

Passenger Cars (large)
State Car Series 1929-35

412   Pullman CALIFORNIA
1. State green/dark green/apple green	(4)	1600
2. State green/dark green/cream	(5)	2200
3. State brown/dk brn-tan vents/cream	(5)	1700
4. State brown/solid dark brown/cream	(5)	2000

413   Pullman COLORADO
1. State green/dark green/apple green	(4)	1600
2. State green/dark green/cream	(5)	2200
3. State brown/dk brn-tan vents/cream	(5)	1700
4. State brown/solid dark brown/cream	(5)	2000

414   Pullman ILLINOIS
1. State green/dark green/apple green	(5)	2000
2. State green/dark green/cream	(5)	3000
3. State brown/dk brn-tan vents/cream	(5)	1800
4. State brown/solid dark brown/cream	(5)	2200

416   Observation NEW YORK
1. State green/dark green/apple green	(4)	1700
2. State green/dark green/cream	(4)	2200
3. State brown/dk brn-tan vents/cream	(5)	1800
4. State brown/solid dark brown/cream	(5)	2000

Blue Comet Series 1930-40

420   Pullman FAYE
1. Medium blue/dark blue/brass	(4)	800
2. Light blue/dark blue/nickel & brass	(4)	900
3. Light blue/dark blue/all nickel	(5)	1200

421   Pullman WESTPHAL
1. Medium blue/dark blue/brass	(4)	800
2. Light blue/dark blue/nickel & brass	(4)	900
3. Light blue/dark blue/all nickel	(5)	1200

422   Observation TEMPEL
1. Medium blue/dark blue/brass	(4)	800
2. Light/blue/dark blue/nickel & brass	(4)	900
3. Light blue/dark blue/all nickel	(5)	1200

Stephen Girard Series 1931-40

424   Pullman LIBERTY BELL
Green/dark green/cream
1. Brass trim	(4)	600
2. Nickel trim	(4)	750

425   Pullman STEPHEN GIRARD
Green/dark green/cream
1. Brass trim	(4)	600
2. Nickel trim	(4)	750

426   Observation CORAL ISLE
Green/dark green/cream
1. Brass trim	(4)	600
2. Nickel trim	(4)	750

418, 419, 431, 490 Series 1923-32

Note: Most stamped New York Central or Lionel Lines. Illinois Central markings are rare.

418 **Pullman** 23-32
1. Mojave/10 series 4w trucks 23-25 (2) 250
2. Mojave/6w trucks 25-33 (3) 275
3. Apple green/apple green/red 29-33 (4) 300

419 **Combine** 23-32
1. Mojave/10 series 4w trucks 23-25 (2) 250
2. Mojave/6w trucks 25-33 (3) 275
3. Apple green/apple green/red 29-33 (4) 300

431 **Diner** 27-32
1. Mojave/6w trucks 27-33 (4) 500
2. Same with hinged roof (5) 1000
3. Apple green/apple green/red 29-33 (5) 600
4. Same as 2 with hinged roof (5) 800

490 **Observation** 23-32
1. Mojave/10 series 4w trucks 23-25 (2) 250
2. Mojave/6w trucks 25-33 (3) 275
3. Apple green/apple green/red 29-33 (4) 300

428, 429, 430 Series 1926-30

Note: Lionel Lines markings

427 **Diner** Never made

428 **Pullman**
1. Dark green/dark green/maroon (2) 350
2. Dark green/dark green/orange (3) 350
3. Orange/orange/SG green (5) 650

429 **Combine**
1. Dark green/dark green/maroon (2) 350
2. Dark green/dark green/orange (3) 350
3. Orange/orange/SG green (5) 650

430 **Observation**
1. Dark green/dark green/maroon (2) 350
2. Dark green/dark green/orange (3) 350
3. Orange/orange/SG green (5) 650

Passenger Cars (medium)

309, 310, 322 Series 1926-40

Note: New York Central or Lionel Lines markings

309 **Pullman**
1. Mojave/mojave/maroon (2) 150
2. Pea green/pea green/orange (1) 125
3. Maroon/terra cotta/cream (5) 250
4. State brown/dark brown/cream (4) 200
5. Medium blue/dark blue/cream (4) 250
6. Stephen Girard green/dk grn/cream (5) 300
7. Light blue/silver/silver (2) 200
8. Red-orange/alum/alum U 5P

310 **Baggage**
1. Mojave/mojave/maroon (2) 150
2. Pea green/pea green/orange (1) 125
3. State brown/dark brown/cream (4) 200
4. Medium blue/dark blue/cream (4) 250
5. Stephen Girard green/dk grn/cream (5) 300
6. Light blue/silver/silver (2) 200
7. Red-orange/alum/alum U 5P

---

312 **Observation**
1. Mojave/mojave/maroon (2) 150
2. Pea green/pea green/orange (1) 125
3. Maroon/terra cotta/cream (5) 250
4. State brown/dark brown/cream (4) 200
5. Medium blue/dark blue/cream (4) 250
6. Stephen Girard green/dk grn/cream (5) 300
7. Light blue/silver/silver (2) 200
8. Red-orange/alum/alum U 5P

319, 320, 322 Series 1924-27

Note: Maroon/maroon/mojave only

319 **Pullman**
1. *New York Central* (2) 100
2. *Illinois Central* (4) 400
3. *Lionel Lines* (2) 100

320 **Baggage** 25-27
1. *New York Central* (2) 100
2. *Illinois Central* (4) 400
3. *Lionel Lines* (3) 150
4. *Lionel Electrical Railroad* (3) 150

322 **Observation**
1. *New York Central* (2) 100
2. *Illinois Central* (4) 400
3. *Lionel Lines* (2) 100

1766, 1767, 1768 Series 1934-40
Lionel Lines Series

1766 **Pullman**
1. Terra cotta/maroon/cream/brass (4) 600
2. Vermilion/maroon/nickel (5) 700

1767 **Baggage**
1. Terra cotta/maroon/cream/brass (4) 600
2. Vermilion/maroon/nickel (5) 700

1768 **Observation**
1. Terra cotta/maroon/cream/brass (4) 600
2. Vermilion/maroon/nickel (5) 700

Passenger Cars (small)

332 **Baggage** 26-33
Note: Came in sets with 337,338 series and 339,341 series.
1. Gray/maroon (2) 100
2. Peacock/orange/orange doors (2) 100
3. Peacock/orange/red doors (3) 125
4. Olive green/red (3) 150
5. Red/cream (3) 150
6. Peacock/dark green/orange (4) 150
7. State brown/dark brown/cream U (5) 300
8. Peacock/orange/red doors w/divider (3) 150
9. Olive/maroon doors (5) *

337, 338 Series 1925-32

337 **Pullman**
1. Mojave/maroon (3) 100
2. Olive green/maroon (1) 100
3. Olive green/red (2) 100
4. Red/cream (3) 150
(also came in Macy's U set)
5. Pea green/cream Macy's U (4) 300

---

338 **Observation**
1. Mojave/maroon (3) 100
2. Olive green/maroon (1) 100
3. Olive green/red (2) 100
4. Red/cream (3) 150
5. Same as 4 with Macy's sticker
on drumhead (4) 300
6. Pea green/cream Macy's U (4) 300

339, 341 Series 1925-33

339 **Pullman**
1. Gray/maroon (2) 100
2. Peacock/orange (1) 100
3. Peacock/dark green/orange (2) 100
4. State brown/dark brown/cream U (5) 300
5. Ives 1694 gray/maroon/cream U (4) 150

341 **Observation**
1. Gray/maroon (2) 100
2. Peacock/orange (1) 100
3. Peacock/dark green/orange (2) 100
4. State brown/dark brown/cream U (5) 300
5. Ives 1694 gray/maroon/cream U (4) 150
Note: Both 337,338 and 339,341 series came with Lionel Lines, New York Central, and Ilinois Central markings. NDV

341 **Observation** (4) 150
RS *THE IVES RAILWAY LINES*
Peacock/dark green/orange

200 Series Freights

211 **Flatcar** 26-40 Black/RS *Lionel Lines* (2) 75

212 **Gondola** 26-40
1. Gray (4) 175
2. Maroon (2) 100
3. Green (3) 100
4. Medium green (4) 150
5. Mojave (4) 175
6. Dark green (5) 275

213 **Cattle Car** 26-40
1. Mojave/maroon (3) 250
2. Terra-cotta/pea green (2) 250
3. Cream/maroon (5) 700
Note: Roofs from 213 and 214 are interchangeable.

214 **Boxcar** 26-40
1. Terra-cotta/dark green (4) 300
2. Cream/orange (2) 250
3. Yellow/brown (3) 500

214R **Refrigerator** 29-40
1. Ivory/peacock (4) 600
2. White/light blue/brass (5) 700
3. White/light blue/nickel (5) 900

215 **Tank** 26-40
1. Pea green (2) 175
2. Ivory/Sunoco decal (3) 225
3. Ivory/no Sunoco decal (3) 300
4. Aluminum/Sunoco decal/brass (4) 400
5. Aluminum/Sunoco decal/nickel (5) 550

216 **Hopper** 26-38 Dark green
  1. Brass (3) 250
  2. Nickel (5) 1000

217 **Caboose** 26-40
  1. Orange/maroon (5) 450
  2. Red/peacock/red cupola (2) 175
  3. Red/peacock/peacock cupola (4) 500
  4. Light red/nickel (4) 250
  5. Pea green/red/brass 5P

218 **Dump** 26-38
  1. Mojave/2 brass knobs/brass ends (3) 225
  2. Mojave/1 brass knob/brass ends (2) 200
  3. Mojave/1 brass knob/mojave ends (2) 200
  4. Green/red/brass ends 1926 5P
  5. Gray/brass ends 5P
  6. Pea green/maroon ends 5P

219 **Derrick** 26-40
  1. Peacock/red boom (2) 200
  2. Yellow/red/green or red boom NDV (4) 300
  3. Ivory/red/green boom (5) 350

220 **Floodlight** 31-40
  1. Terra-cotta/brass lights (2) 250
  2. Green/nickel-plated lights (3) 300

500 Series Freights

511 **Flat Car** 27-39
  1. Dark green/gold RS lettering (1) 50
  2. Medium green/silver RS lettering (3) 60
  3. Medium green/gold RS lettering (2) 60
  Note: Brakewheel placed differently through the years. NDV

512 **Gondola** 27-39
  1. Peacock (1) 50
  2. Green (2) 50

513 **Cattle Car** 27-38
  1. Olive green/orange (3) 125
  2. Orange/pea green (2) 100
  3. Cream/maroon (5) 500

514 **Boxcar** 29-40
  1. Cream/orange (2) 150
  2. Yellow/brown (3) 175

514 **Refrigerator** 27,28
  Ivory/peacock (3) 225

514R **Refrigerator** 29-40
  1. Ivory/peacock (3) 225
  2. White/light blue (5) 500

515 **Tank** 27-40
  1. Terra cotta/no decal (2) 150
  2. Ivory/no Sunoco decal (2) 150
  3. Ivory/Sunoco decal (3) 175
  4. Alum/Sunoco decal (3) 175
  5. Tan w & w/o Sunoco decal (4) 175
  6. Shell orange/Shell decal (5) 800
  Note: Brakewheel on left side on early versions; right side on later versions. NDV

516 **Hopper** 28-40
  1. Red/no coal load/brass (1) 150
  2. Red/coal load/brass (2) 250
  3. Red/coal load/RS capacity lettering (4) 275
  4. Red/coal load/nickel (5) 375

517 **Caboose** 27-40
  1. Pea green/red/brass (2) 100
  2. Pea green/red/orange (2) 100
  3. Red/black/orange (5) 850
  4. Red/aluminum (4) 250
  5. Red/alum/no number plates; (4) 500
    number rubber-stamped on bottom

520 **Floodlight** 31-40
  1. Terra-cotta/brass lights (1) 150
  2. Green/nickel plated lights (2) 175
  Early: brakewheel left. Late: right. NDV

Trolleys

Note: All 1, 2, 3, and 4 series trolleys and trailers had number plus Electric Rapid Transit on side, except when indicated.

1 **Trolley** 06 4-wheels 5 window, no reverse, no headlight/smooth sides
  New Departure Motor Orange/cream (5) 3000

1 **Trailer** 07 5 window
  Blue/cream (5) 2500

1 **Trolley** 08 6 window
  Embossed sides/standard motor
  1. Blue/cream (4) 2500
  2. Dark green/cream (5) 3000

1 **Trailer** 08 6 windows blue/cream (3) 2000

1 **Trolley** 10-14 6 window
  Used 1908/09 version of 2 trolley body
  1. Blue/cream (4) 2500
  2. Blue/cream *Curtis Bay* (5) 3000

2 **Trolley** 06-14 4-wheels headlight and reverse
  1. Cream/red/open ends 06 (5) 2000
  2. Blue/cream windows/open ends 08 (4) 2000
  3. Red/cream windows (4) 2000
    closed offset ends 10-12
  4. Dark olive green/orange windows (5) 2200
    closed flush ends 13-16
  5. Cream/red/closed flush ends (4) 1800

2 **Trailer**
200 1. Cream/red/matches no. 1 above (5) 1800
  2. Red/cream/matches no. 3 above (4) 1500

3 **Trolley** 06-13 8-wheels
  1. Cream/dk olive green/flat windows (5) 3000
    open ends 1906
  2. Cream/dk olive green/inset windows (5) 3000
    open ends 1908
  3. Cream/orange/open ends (5) 3000
    inset windows 1908
  4. Orange/cream/open ends (5) 3000
    inset windows 1908
  5. Dark olive green/cream/closed (5) 3000
    offset ends 1910
  6. Dark olive green/cream/closed flush (5) 3000
    ends 1913
  7. Same but lettered *Bay Shore* (5) 3000

3 **Trailer** 08 (5) 2800
300 Matches nos. 2,3, and 4

4 **Trolley** 06-13 8 wheels
  Same body as 3 but with 2 motors - early
  1. Dk olive green/cream/ (5) 5000
    open ends - late
  2. Dark olive green/cream/flush ends (5) 5000

8 **Trolley** 09-15 *PAY AS YOU ENTER*
  8-wheels single motor
  1. Cream/orange/9 windows (5) 6000
  2. Dark olive green/cream 11 windows (5) 6000

9 **Trolley** 09-12 *PAY AS YOU ENTER*
  8-wheels double motor
  1. Cream/orange/9 windows (5) 6000
  2. Dark olive green/cream/11 windows (5) 6000

10 **Interurban** 10-16
1010 **Trailer**
  1. Maroon/gold/high knobs (5) 4000
  2. Dark olive green/low knobs (4) 3000
  3. Dark olive green/no knobs (4) 1500
  4. Same but RS *WB&A* *
    Both powered and trailer
    units stamped 1010

100 **Trolley** 1910 5 windows
  Blue/cream (4) 2000
1000 **Trailer** matches 100 (4) 1500

100 **Trolley** 13-14 5 windows
  1. Red/cream (4) 2000
  2. Blue/cream (4) 2000
  3. Blue/cream/lettered *Linden Ave* (5) 4000

1000 **Trailer** matches nos. 1 and 2 (4) 1500
1000 **Trailer** *Linden Ave* (5) 3500

100 **Trolley** 14-16 6 windows
  1. Red/cream (4) 2000
  2. Blue/cream (4) 2000
1000 **Trailer** matches 100 (4) 1500

101 **Open Summer Trolley** 10-13 four wheels
  1. Blue roof and ends (4) 2000
  2. Same but lettered *101 Wilkins Ave* (5) 2500
  3. Red roof and ends (4) 2000
1100 **Trailer** matches 101

202 **Open Summer Trolley** 10-13 4-wheels
  Red/cream/black (5) 3000
2200 **Trailer** matches 202 (5) 2500

303 **Open Summer Trolley** 10-13 8-wheels
  Green/cream/maroon (5) 3000

3300 **Trailer** matches 303 (5) 2500

Early Period
Standard Gauge 1906-1926

Steamers

5   **0-4-0** 06-26 black no tender
    1. Thin rims   (4) 700
    2. Thick rims   (3) 500

5   **Special 0-4-0** 06-11 thin rims
    1. 4w tender/10 series solid   (5) 1000
       3-rivet truck
    2. 4w tender/10 series open   (4) 900
       3-rivet truck
    3. 8w tender 2 100 series trucks   (4) 700

51   **0-4-0** 12-23 thick rims   (3) 700
    6w tender 2 100 series trucks
    Note: 5, 5 Special and the 51 are the same loco

6   **4-4-0** 06-23 black/nickel trim 8w tender
    1. Thin rims   (4) 1500
    2. Thick rims   (3) 1200

6   **Special 4-4-0** 08,09 brass/nickel   (5) 2000
    8w tender/ thin rims
    Note: 6, 6 Special and 7 are the same loco

7   **4-4-0** 10-23 brass/nickel 8w tender
    1. Thin rims/open 3- rivet trucks   (5) 3000
    2. Thick rims/singl- rivet trucks   (4) 2500
    Note: In general, thin rims and split frames are
    more desirable than thick rims and solid frames.

Electrics

33   **0-6-0 Round Cab** 1913 only (first versions)
    1. Dark olive green/*NYC* oval   (2) 600
    2. Dark olive green/block *Penn RR*   (5) 900
    3. Dark olive green/red stripe   (4) 700
    4. Black   (4) 700

33   **0-4-0 Round Cab** 13-24 (second versions)
    NYC markings: common. *C&O* markings: rare.
    1. Dark olive green   (2) 125
    2. Midnight blue DSS   (5) 2000
    3. Black   (2) 125
    4. Gray   (2) 125
    5. Maroon   (4) 500
    6. Red   (4) 500
    7. Peacock   (4) 600
    8. Dark green   (3) 200
    9. Red with cream striping   (4) 600
    10. Brown   (4) 500
    11. Mojave   (3) 300
    12. Pea green   (4) 400
    13. Black FAOS DSS 1915   (5) 2000

34   **0-6-0 Round Cab** 12, U13   (4) 900
    Dark olive green RS block *NYC* or *NYC* oval

38   **0-4-0 Round Cab** 13-24 RS *NYC* oval or block
    lettering
    1. Dark olive green   (3) 250
    2. Black   (2) 150
    3. Maroon   (3) 300
    4. Dark green   (3) 400
    5. Mojave   (4) 500
    6. Peacock   (5) 800
    7. Gray   (2) 150
    8. Brown   (3) 300
    9. Red/cream stripe   (4) 600
    10. Red   (4) 700
    11. Dark olive green/RS *Penn RR*   (4) 600
    12. Black *FAOS* 62 DSS   (5) 1000

42   **0-4-4-0 Square Cab** 1912 dark green
    NYC oval or block lettering
    1. Thin rims   (5) 1600
    2. Thick rims   (4) 1500

42   **0-4-4 Round Cab** 13-23 *NYC* oval or block
    lettering
    1. Black   (2) 500
    2. Maroon   (5) 2000
    3. Dark gray   (3) 700
    4. Dark green   (3) 700
    5. Mojave   (4) 800
    6. Peacock   (5) 1800
    7. Gray   (2) 500
    8. Olive green   (4) 1200
    9. Pea green   (4) 1200
    10. "61 FAOS" DSS 1915   (5) 2500
    Note: Odd colors turn up as a result
    of Lionel's policy of repainting trains
    which were sent in for repair.

50   **0-4-0 Round Cab** 1924 only
    Standard motor version:
    1. Dark gray   (2) 150
    2. Dark green   (3) 200
    3. Maroon   (4) 400
    Super motor version:
    1. Dark gray   (2) 150
    2. Mojave   (4) 400
    3. Dark green   (3) 200

53   **0-4-4-0 Square Cab** 12-14
    Script *NYNH&H*, oval or block *NYC*
    1. Maroon   (4) 1500
    2. Brown   (4) 1500

53   **0-4-0 Square Cab** 15-19 *NYC* oval
    1. Maroon   (2) 800
    2. Dark olive green   (4) 1200
    3. Mojave   (4) 1000

53   **0-4-0 Round Cab** 20,21 *NYC* oval   (4) 1000
    Maroon

54   **0-4-4-0 Square Cab** 1912 only   (5) 3500
    Pedestal type headlight/thick rim drivers

54   **0-4-4-0 Round Cab** 13-24
    Same as 42 but brass body, red spokes, and
    ventilators, red cab door window frames.
    1. Single motor   (4) 2500
    2. Double motor   (5) 2800

1910   **0-6-0 Square Cab** 10,11 *NYNH&H*   (4) 1500
    Dark olive green

1910   **0-6-0 Round Cab** 1912 only *NYC* oval (3) 1000
    Dark olive green

1911   **0-4-0 Square Cab** 10,11 *NYC* oval or block
    NYNH&H
    1. Maroon   (5) 2000
    2. Dark olive green   (4) 1800
    Note: Add $200 for thick-rim version

1911   **0-4-0 Round Cab** 1912 only   (3) 1200
    NYNH&H or block NYC dark olive green

1911   **0-4-4-0 Special Square Cab** 11,12   (5) 2000
    Dark olive green/block *NYC*

1912   **0-4-4-0 Square Cab** 10-12
    Dark olive green
    1. Thin rims/script *NYNH&H*   (5) 3500
    2. Thick rims/block *NYC*   (4) 3300

1912   **0-4-4-0 Special Square Cab**   (4) 5000
    1911 only/ same as 1912 but made of brass
    Note: In general square cabs and thin-rims are
    more desirable than round bodies and thick rims.
    Only exception is the 1911 with thick rims.

Passenger Cars

Note: Price listed is per car

18,19,190 Series 06-27
    1. Dark olive green/red window trim
      High knobs   (5) 1800
      Low knobs   (5) 1800
      No knobs   (3) 200
    2. Yellow orange   (4) 750
    3. Dark orange   (3) 200
    4. Mojave   (4) 700

29   **Day Coach** 08-21
    Early 08,09
    Same body as No. 3 trolley.   (5) 2000
    NYC & HRRR or *Pennsylvania RR*.
    Closed or open ends. Solid steps.
    Middle 10,11
    High knobs or low knobs. *NYC&HRRR*
    perforated or 3-hole steps
    1. Maroon/black trim   (5) 2000
    2. Dark green   (5) 2000
    Late 12-21
    Open clerestory, 3-hole steps, removable roof
    1. Dark olive green/maroon stripe   (4) 1500
    2. Dark olive green/no maroon stripe   (4) 1500

31 Combine, 32 Baggage 21-25
35 Pullman, 36 Observation 12-26
RS *NYC* common
RS *C&O* or *NYNH&H* rare
1. Green	(2)	85
2. Dark blue DSS	(5)	250
3. Orange	(4)	150
4. Maroon	(3)	85
5. Brown	(3)	85
6. Dark olive green	(2)	75

180,181,182 Series 11-21
1. Maroon early	(5)	250
2. Maroon late	(3)	150
3. Brown	(4)	200

1910 09,10 RS 1910 and Pullman
Open 3-rivet trucks 3 high knobs
Green	(5)	1800

10 Series Freights

11 Flat 06-26
Cars RS *Pennsylvania RR* rare
1. Orange DSS	(5)	250
2. Red	(3)	75
3. Brown	(2)	75
4. Maroon handrails	(4)	125
5. Maroon no handrails	(2)	75
6. Gray DSS	(4)	150
7. Dark olive green	(3)	75

12 Gondola 06-26
RS *Lake Shore* or *Rock Island*
1. Red	(4)	75
2. Brown	(4)	75
3. Gray	(4)	75
4. Maroon	(4)	75

Note: Early versions have brakewheel outside and flat edges. Later versions have brakewheel inside and rolled edges. Add $100 for early versions.

13 Cattle 06-26 various shades of green
Early Five slats/smooth surface/ two-piece roof/*Lionel Mfg.*	(5)	300
Middle 6 slats/embossed surface/ one-piece roof/*Lionel Corp*	(3)	75
Late 6 slats/embossed surface/ no brakewheel/*Lionel Corp*	(3)	75

14 Box 06-26
1. Red/smooth sides	(5)	350
2. Red/embossed sides	(4)	300
3. Yellow-orange/embossed sides	(3)	100
4. Orange/embossed sides	(2)	75
5. Dk olive grn/embossed sides DSS	(4)	250

14 Harmony Creamery 1921 only
Dark green
	5+

15 Oil Tank 06-26
1. Red/wood domes, ends/U-shaped wire step/RS *416 Pennsylvania*	(5)	350
2. Wine/three-piece step/metal ends	(4)	200
3. Wine or brown/single step with three holes/metal ends	(2)	75

16 Ballast 06-26
1. Gray	(5)	400
2. Brown	(3)	200
3. Red	(3)	200
4. Dark green	(3)	200
5. Wine	(2)	150

17 Caboose 06-26
Early Smooth sides/awnings over main windows/no cupola awnings/vertical striping/steps formed from platform
Middle Embossed sides/no awnings over main windows/awnings over cupola windows/steps formed from platform
Late Embossed sides/no awnings over cupola or main windows/soldered on 3-hole steps/rounded windows rather than square
1. Red/black roof	(5)	350
2. Brown/black roof	(3)	150
3. Wine/black roof	(2)	75

100 Series Freights

112 Gondola 10-26
Early 10-12 (7-inches long)
1. Dark olive green/red RS *Lake Shore* or *NYNH&H*	(5)	300

Middle 13-26 (9 1/2-inches long)
2. Red/dark olive green trim	(4)	150
3. Maroon	(3)	75
4. Brown	(3)	75
5. Dark gray	(2)	50
6. Gray	(3)	50
7. Orange	(5)	200

113 Cattle 12-26
	(3)	50

Green/embossed sides/no lettering
Note: Early cars are darker green than later cars.

114 Box 12-26
1. Red	(4)	150
2. Yellow-orange	(3)	75
3. Orange	(2)	50
4. Dark olive green DSS	(5)	150

116 Ballast 10-26
1. Dark olive green	(5)	75
2. Maroon	(4)	65
3. Brown	(2)	50
4. Dark gray	(2)	50
5. Gray	(2)	50
6. Dark green	(3)	50

117 Caboose 12-26
RS *NYC&HRRR* 4351
1. Red/black roof	(5)	75
2. Brown/black roof	(4)	65
3. Maroon/black roof	(3)	50

Note: Most desirable items in the Early Period are extremely rare. In some cases, less than 10 are known to exist. Therefore, rarity ratings indicate relative rarity and desirability to other items within the Early Period.

2 7/8-Inch Gauge

Note: These were the first trains Joshua Lionel Cowen made. They are extremely rare. About 30 collectible variations exist. The largest known 2 7/8-inch gauge collection has nine pieces. Few items in this category are ever sold so the prices listed are estimates. All metal and iron cars have black frames, 4 wheels, and Lionel Manufacturing Company stamped on floor. Reproductions exist.

100 Electric Locomotive 01-05
	(5)	4000
1. Maroon/black roof		
2. Apple green		

200 Electric Express 01-05
1. Electric Express/wooden car body no corner braces	(5)	6000
2. Same with corner braces	(5)	5000
3. Sheet-metal body/maroon	(5)	5000
4. Sheet-metal body/apple green	(5)	5000

300 Electric Trolley 01-05
	(5)	5000

Maroon/light green/6 reversible seats, lettered *City Hall Park* on one end and *Union Depot* on the other

309 Trolley Trailer 01-05 matches 300

400 Express Trailer matches 200
	(5)	3000
1. Gold RS lettering *Lake Shore*		
2. Green/gold RS lettering *B&O*		

500 Electric Derrick 03,04
	(5)	3000

Maroon/black derrick made of cast iron, brass chain with tackle attached

600 Derrick Trailer 03,04
Same as 500 but without motor

800 Electric Box 04,05
	(5)	3000

Maroon/maroon roof/gold RS lettering *Metropolitan Express*

900 Electric Box Trailer 04,05
	(5)	3000

Matches 800

1000 Electric Passenger 05
	(5)	5000
1. Maroon/black roof/gold RS lettering *Metropolitan St. R.R. CO.*		
2. Same as 1 but lettered *Maryland St. RY Co.*		

1050 Passenger Trailer 04,05
	(5)	5000

Matches 1000
1. Maroon/black roof/gold RS lettering *Metropolitan St. R.R. Co.*
2. Lettered *Maryland St. RY Co.*
3. Lettered *Philadelphia R.T. Co.*

OO Gauge

Locomotives

001	**Hudson** 4-6-4 38-42 Scale Fully detailed/3-rail/RS 5342		
	1. 001T no whistle	(3)	400
	2. 001W with whistle	(3)	425
002	**Hudson** 4-6-4 39-42 Modified Semi-detailed/3-rail/RS 5342		
	1. 002T no whistle	(4)	350
	2. 002W with whistle	(4)	375
003	**Hudson** 4-6-4 39-42 Scale Fully detailed/2-rail/RS 5342		
	1. 003T no whistle	(4)	425
	2. 003W with whistle	(4)	450
004	**Hudson** 4-6-4 39-42 Modified Semi-detailed/2-rail/RS 5342		
	1. 004T no whistle	(5)	350
	2. 004W with whistle	(5)	375
0081K	**Kit** containing 001 and 001T	(5)	500
0081KW	**Kit** containing 001 and 001W	(5)	500

Rolling Stock

0014	**Box** 38-42 Detailed 3-rail		
	1. Orange/decal *Lionel Lines* 38	(4)	100
	2. Yellow/maroon roofwalk/decal *Lionel Lines* 38	(4)	100
	3. Tuscan/decal *Pennsylvania* 39-42	(3)	75
0015	**Tank** 38-42 Detailed 3-rail		
	1. Silver/*Sunoco* U38	(4)	50
	2. Black/*Shell* 39,40,42	(3)	50
	3. Gray/*Shell* 39,40,42	(3)	50
	4. Black/*Sunoco* 41	(5)	100
0016	**Hopper** 38-42 Detailed 3-rail		
	1. Gray/*SP* U38	(4)	100
	2. Black/*SP* 39-42	(4)	100
0017	**Caboose** 38-42 Detailed 3-rail		
	1. Red/*NYC* 38-42	(3)	50
	2. Red/maroon roofwalk/*PRR* 40	(4)	75
0024	**Box** 39-42 Semi-detailed 3-rail Tuscan/*Pennsylvania*	(3)	50
0025	**Tank** 39-42 Semi-detailed 3-rail		
	1. Black/*Shell* 39-42	(3)	50
	2. Black/*Sunoco* 41	(4)	75
0027	**Caboose** 39-42 Semi-detailed 3-rail		
	1. Red/*NYC*	(3)	50
	2. Red/maroon roofwalk/*PRR* 41	(4)	75
0044	**Box** 39-42 Detailed 2-rail Tuscan/*Pennsylvania*	(3)	50
0044K	**Box Kit** 39-42 Semi-detailed 2 or 3 rail Tuscan/*Pennsylvania*	(4)	75

0045	**Tank** 39-42 Detailed 2-rail		
	1. Black/*Shell* 39,40-42	(3)	50
	2. Black/*Sunoco* 41	(4)	75
0045K	**Tank Kit** 39-42 Semi-detailed 2 or 3 rail		
	1. Black/*Shell* 39,40,42	(4)	75
	2. Black/*Sunoco* 41	(4)	75
0046	**Hopper** 39-42 Detailed 2-rail Black/*SP*	(3)	50
0047	**Caboose** 39-42 Detailed 2-rail		
	1. Red/*NYC* 39-42	(3)	50
	2. Red/maroon roofwalk/*PRR* 40	(3)	50
0047K	**Caboose** Kit 39-42 Semi-detailed 2 or 3 rail		
	1. Red/*NYC* 39-42	(3)	75
	2. Red/maroon roofwalk/*PRR* 40	(4)	75
0074	**Box** 39-42 Semi-detailed 2-rail Tuscan/*Pennsylvania*	(3)	50
0075	**Tank** 39-42 Semi-detailed 2-rail		
	1. Silver/*Sunoco* U39	(4)	100
	2. Black/*Shell* 39,40,42		
	3. Black/*Sunoco* 41		
0077	**Caboose** 39-42 Semi-detailed 2-rail		
	1. Red/*NYC* 39-42	(3)	50
	2. Red/maroon roofwalk/decal *PRR* 40	(4)	50

Track & Transformers

Standard Gauge Track

S	**12" Straight Track** 3 ties 07,08	(5)	10
S	**14" Straight Track** 3 ties 08-30	(3)	4
S	**14" Straight Track** 31-42 4 ties	(2)	2
SC	**14" Straight Track** 15-22 with electrical connections, 3 ties	(4)	10
20	**90 Degree Crossing** 09-42		
	1. Depressed center	(4)	5
	2. Fibre center and solid metal base	(2)	5
	3. Bakelite center and solid metal base	(2)	5
20X	**45 Degree Crossing** 28-32	(3)	10
21	**90 Degree Crossing** 1906	(4)	10
21	**Manual Switch** Illuminated		
	1. No fibre rails 15-22	(3)	20
	2. Fibre rails 23-25	(4)	25
22	**Manual Switch** 06-22		
	1. Cast iron switch stand 06-15	(3)	20
	2. Stamped steel switch stand 16-22	(2)	20
22	**Manual Switch** 23-25 with fibre rails	(3)	20
23	**Bumper** 15-33	(3)	25
25	**Bumper** 27-42 Black/yellow-red	(3)	27

210	**Pair of Switches** 26-42 Right and left hand		
	1. Green base 26-33	(3)	30
	2. Black base 34-42	(2)	30
210L	**Manual Switch** 26-42 Left hand	(2)	20
210R	**Manual Switch** 26-42 Right hand	(2)	20
220	**Pair of Manual Switches** 26 No light	(2)	15
222	**Pair of Manual Switches** 26-32 Illuminated	(3)	40
222L	**Left-Hand Switch** 26-32 Illuminated	(2)	20
222R	**Right-Hand Switch** 26-32 Illuminated	(2)	20
223	**Pair of N-D Switches** 32-42 Illuminated		
	1. Green base	(4)	75
	2. Black base	(4)	75
223L	**Left-Hand N-D Switch** 32-42 Illuminated	(4)	35
223R	**Right-Hand N-D Switch** 32-42 Illuminated	(4)	35
225	**439 Control Panel** 29-32 with 222 switches	(4)	200

OO Gauge Track, Crossings, and Switches

OO-31	**Curved Track** 39-42 2-rail	(4)	10
OO-32	**Straight Track** 39-42 2-rail	(5)	25
OO-34	**Curved Track** 39-42 2-rail	(4)	15
OO-51	**Curved Track** 39-42 3-rail	(3)	5
OO-52	**Straight Track** 39-42 3-rail	(4)	10
OO-54	**Curved Track** 39-42 3-rail with electrical connections	(3)	5
OO-61	**Curved Track** 38 3-rail	(3)	5
OO-62	**Straight Track** 38 3-rail	(4)	10
OO-63	**Curved Track** 38-42 3-rail 1/2 section	(5)	10
OO-64	**Curved Track** 38 with electrical connections	(3)	5
OO-65	**Straight Track** 38-42 3-rail 1/2 section	(5)	15
OO-66	**Straight Track** 38-42 3-rail 5/6 section	(5)	25
OO-70	**90 Degree Crossing** 38-42	(3)	5
OO-72	**Switches** 38-42 3-rail pair	(4)	75
OO-72L	**Switch** 38-42 3-rail	(4)	35
OO-72R	**Switch** 38-42 3-rail	(4)	35

Transformers and Controllers

Note: All transformers are for 110 volt, 60 cycle current, unless otherwise noted.

A	**Transformer** 22-37		
	1. 40 Watts 22-31	(3)	5
	2. 60 Watts 32-37	(1)	10
B	**Transformer** 17-38		
	1. 50 Watts 17	(4)	5
	2. 75 Watts 18-38	(1)	7
C	**Transformer** 22-37	(5)	5
	75 Watts 25-40 cycle		
F	**Transformer** 30-37	(5)	5
	40 Watts 25-40 cycle		
H	**Transformer** 38-39	(5)	5
	75 Watts 25-40 cycle		
J	**Transformer** U36 100 Watts 4 current	(5)	5
	selection: 90-250 volt/40-133 cycle		
K	**Transformer** 15-38		
	1. 200 Watts cast iron case	(3)	25
	slate top 15-19		
	2. 150 Watts sheet-metal	(1)	20
	case & top 20-38		
L	**Transformer** 14,35-38		
	1. 75 Watts brass case slate top 14	(4)	8
	2. 50 Watts black sheet-metal	(1)	5
	case & top 35-38		
	3. 50 Watts red sheet-metal	(4)	5
	case & top		
N	**Transformer** 42 50 Watts	(3)	5

Q	**Transformer** 39-42 75 Watts	(2)	5
R	**Transformer** 39-42 100 Watts	(1)	5
T	**Transformer** 15-38		
	1. 75 Watts 15-17	(4)	5
	2. 150 Watts 18-21	(5)	5
	3. 110 Watts 22	(5)	8
	4. 100 Watts 23-38	(1)	5
U	**Transformer** 33 50 Watts	(3)	40
V	**Transformer** 39-41 150 Watts	(2)	50
W	**Transformer** 39-42 75 Watts	(3)	10
Z	**Transformer** 39-42 250 Watts	(4)	200
65	**Whistle Controller** 35	(4)	10
66	**Whistle Controller** 36-39	(1)	5
67	**Whistle Controller** 36-39	(1)	5
81	**Controlling Rheostat** 27-33	(2)	5
88	**Battery Rheostat** 15-28	(3)	5
91	**Circuit Breaker** 30-42	(1)	5
95	**Controlling Rheostat** 34-42	(2)	5
96C	**Control Button** 38-42	(1)	5
167	**Whistle Controller** 40-42	(1)	10
167X	**Whistle Controller** OO 40-42	(3)	25
168	**Magic-Electrol Controller** 40-42	(3)	30

169	**Teledyne Controller** 40-42	(3)	30
170	**Direct Current Reducer** 14-38	(5)	10
	220 Volt		
171	**Direct Current Inverter** 36-42	(3)	10
	115 Volt		
172	**Direct Current Inverter** 37-42	(5)	10
	220 Volt		
1012	**Station Transformer** 30-32	(4)	30
	Winner Lines		
1017	**Station Transformer** 33	(3)	50
1027	**Station Transformer** 34	(2)	50
1028	**Transformer** 35 25 Watts	(3)	25
1029	**Transformer** 36-37 25 Watts	(1)	5
1030	**Transformer** 36-37 50 Watts	(1)	5
1037	**Transformer** 41-42 40 Watts	(1)	4
1038	**Transformer** U37 30 Watts	(3)	4
1039	**Transformer** 38-40 35 Watts	(1)	3
1040	**Transformer** 39 60 Watts	(1)	15
1041	**Transformer** 40-42 60 Watts	(1)	15
1229	**Transformer** U36 25 Watts 220 volt	(5)	25
1230	**Transformer** U36 50 Watts 220 volt	(5)	25
1239	**Transformer** U38 30 Watts 220 volt	(5)	25

Important Dates

1901	Lionel begins to manufacture toy trains in 2 7/8-inch gauge
1902	Earliest known catalog
1905	Lionel introduces Standard gauge
1905	Mario Caruso starts with Lionel
1906	Lionel Manufacturing Company organized
1908	Operating headlight introduced
1910	Ives catalogs electric trains for the first time
1910-18	Pedestal headlights
1911	Solid frame adopted for locomotives
1912	Thick rims drivers replace thin rims
1915-25	Early rubber-stamped (RS) lettering
1918-26	Nickel-plated strap headlights
1915	Lionel first cataloged O gauge
1918	Lionel Manufacturing becomes Corporation
1924-30	Nickel journals
1925	Two-position reverse E unit introduced
1926	First automatic reversing unit
1928	Until 1928, passenger cars had real railroad names. After 1928, only *Lionel Lines* used.
1926-34	Brass number plates
1927-36	Diecast headlights
1928	Ives files bankruptcy
1929	New Standard gauge steamers introduced
1931-34	Copper journals
1933	Three-position reverse E unit adopted
1933-36	Chugger units in steam locos
1931-34	Copper journals
1934	Lionel placed in receivership
1934	Mickey Mouse handcar introduced
1935	Receivership discharged
1935	Nickel plates and journals
1935	Whistle in tender introduced
1936	Last year electrics were cataloged
1935	Streamline steamers introduced
1938	Automatic box couplers introduced
1937	Scale Hudson introduced
1938	Automatic box coupler introduced
1938	A.C. Gilbert takes over American Flyer
1938	OO gauge introduced
1939	"E" designation dropped on most engines
1939	Standard gauge cataloged for the last time
1940-42	Late rubber-stamped (RS) lettering, black journals
1942	End of prewar O gauge production

Sources

Appraisals

Frank Petruzzo
1-708-301-2896

TM Books & Video
1-219-879-2822

Auctions

Christie's
219 East 67th Street
New York, New York 10021
212-606-0543

Ted Mauer
1931 North Charlotte Street
Pottstown, Pa. 19464

Lloyd Ralston Gallery
173 Post Road
Fairfield, Ct. 06430
203-255-1233

Sotheby's
1334 York Ave.
New York, New York 10021
212-6067424

Books and Magazines

Carstens Publications
PO Box 700
Newton, New Jersey 07860
201-383-3355

Chilton Book Co.
201 King of Prussia Road
Radnor, Pa. 19089

Garden Railways
PO Box 61461
Denver, Co. 80206
1-303-733-4779

Kalmbach Publishing
PO Box 1612
Waukesha, Wis. 53187

O Gauge Railroading
PO Box 239
Nazareth, Pa. 18064

S-Gaugian
Heimberger Publishing Co.
7236 West Madison Street
Forest Park, Ill. 60130

TM Books and Video
Box 279
New Buffalo, Mi. 49117
1-800-892-2822

Trainmaster
PO Box 1499
Gainesville, Fla. 32602

Electronics

Dallee Electronics
10 Witmer Road
Lancaster, Pa. 17602

Depotronics
PO Box 2093
Warrendale, Pa. 15086
412-776-4061

QSI Industries Inc.
2575 Kathryn St. #25
Hillsboro, Oregon 97124
503-591-5786

Ott Machine Services
118 East Ash Street
Lombard, Ill. 60148

Layout Construction

Don Cardiff
St Charles, Ill.

Create-A-Pike
Barillaro Trains
19 Sillmanville Road
Colchester, Ct. 06415

Clark Dunham
Stonebridge Road
Pottersville, New York 12860
518-494-3688

Don Danuser
Box 62
Hood, Va. 22723
703-948-4279

Huff & Puff Industries, Ltd.
24153 Arrowhead Lane
Barrington, Ill. 60010
708-381-8255

Layouts Unlimited, Inc.
PO Box 926
Valley Stream, New York 11580
516-593-1580

Manufacturers

Aristo-Craft
346 Bergen Ave.
Jersey City, New Jersey 07304

Bachmann Industries
1400 East Erie Ave.
Philadelphia, Pa. 19124
215-533-1600

Bowser Manufacturing
21 Howard Street
Montoursville, Pa. 17754

K-Line Electric Trains
PO Box 2831
Chapel Hill, North Carolina 27515
800-866-9986

LGB of America
6444 Nancy Ridge Drive
San Diego, Ca. 92121

Lionel Trains, Inc.
50625 Richard W Blvd.
Chesterfield, Michigan 48051
313-949-4100

Marketing Corp. of America
Box 225
Birmingham, Michigan 48012
313-288-5155

Marklin Inc.
PO Box 51319
New Berlin, Wis. 53151

Marx Trains
c/o Jim Flynn
209 East Butterfield Road
Suite 228
Elmhurst, Ill. 60126
708-941-3843

McCoy Manufacturing
PO Box 444
Kent, Washington 98032
206-852-5595

MTH Electric Trains
9693 Gerwig Lane
Columbia, Md. 21046

Pride Lines
651 West Hoffman Ave.
Lindenhurst, New York 11757
516-225-0033

Putt Trains
PO Box 463
Orwell, Ohio 44076

Red Caboose
PO Box 2490
Longmont, Co. 80502
303-772-8813

Right-of-Way Industries
1145 Highbrook Street
Akron, Ohio 44301
216-535-9200

Charles Ro Supply Co.
347 Pleasant Street
Malden, Ma. 02148

Third Rail
138 West Cambell Ave.
Cambell, Ca. 95008
408-866-1727

Toy Train Historical Foundation
20700 Ventura Blvd.
Suite 205
Woodland Hills, Ca. 91364

Train Express
4365 West 96th Street
Indianapolis, Indiana 46268
317-879-9300

Weaver Models
177 Wheatley Ave.
Northumberland, Pa. 17857

Williams Electric Trains
8835 F-Columbia Parkway
Columbia, Md. 21045
410-997-7766

Charles C. Wood
PO Box 179
Hartford, Ohio 44424
216-772-5177

Miscellaneous

Christopher Enterprises Signals
32 Alexander Blvd.
Poughkeepsie, New York 12603

Mainline Roadbed
PO Box 21861
Chattanooga, Tn. 37241

Moondog Track Patterns
1245 Riverview Drive
Fallbrook, Ca. 92028

O Gauge Template
109 Medallion Center
Dallas, Texas 75214
214-373-9469

Rail Rax Display
786 Seely Ave.
Aromas, Ca. 95004

Rick Johnson Rubber Roadbed
19333 Sturgess Drive
Torrance, Ca. 90503
310-371-3887

Semaphore Locomotive Works
3801 Monarch Drive
Racine, Wisconsin 53406

Mobil Displays

Great Train Shows, Inc.
PO Box 126
Cochranton, Pa. 16314
814-425-3696

Operating Layouts

All Aboard S-Gauge Railroad
1952 Landis Valley Road
Lancaster, Pa. 17601
717-393-0850

Carnegie Science Center
Pittsburgh, Pa. 15212
412-237-3337

Children's Museum
Indianapolis, Indiana

Choo Choo Barn
Rt. 741
Strasburg, Pa. 17575

Entertrainment
Mall of America
Bloomington, Minn. 55425
612-851-9211

Lionel Visitors Center
Chesterfield, Michigan
313-949-4100

Lionel Railroad Club
10236 West Fond du Lac Ave.
Milwaukee, Wis. 53223
414-353-8840

Lionel Railroad Club
c/o Gary Muller
9212 Dana Dale Ct.
St. Louis, Mo. 63123
314-631-0233

Lionel Railroad Club
c/o Tom Wilburn
739 Linden Court
San Bruno, Ca. 94066
415-588-5535

Train Collectors Museum
Paradise Lane
Strasburg, Pa. 17575

Museum of Science & Industry
Chicago, Ill.

Roadside America
Roadside Drive
Shartlesville, Pa. 19554
215-488-6241

Trainland USA
Colfax, Iowa 50054
515-674-3813

Valley Junction Train Station & Museum
401 Railroad Place
West Des Moines, Iowa 50625
515-274-4424

Parts

Alfra Engineering
7910 Poplar Hill Drive
Clinton, Md. 20735

Steve Lukefahr
St. Louis, Mo.

Madison Hardware
1915 West Fort Street
Detroit, Mi. 48216
313-965-9888

Charles Schmidt Trains
Annapolis, Md.

Warren's Model Trains
20520 Lorain Rd.
Fairview Park, Ohio 44126
216-331-2900

Track

The A.C. Valu Toy Co.
3530-25 Long Beach Road
Oceanside, New York 11572

Curtis Hi-Rail Products
PO Box 385
North Stonington, Ct. 06359

Gargraves Trackage Corp.
Box 255-A
North Rose, New York 14516
315-483-6577

Railway Design Associates
241 Silver Street
Monson, Ma. 01057

Rydin Industries, Inc.
28W 215 Warrenville Road
Warrenville, Il. 60555
708-393-1554

Train Clubs

American Flyer Collectors Club
PO Box 13269
Pittsburgh, Pa. 15243

Lionel Operating Train Society
Box 62240
Cincinnati, Ohio 45241

Lionel Collectors Club of America
PO Box 479
La Salle, Ill. 61301

National Association of S Gaugers
c/o Mike Ferraro
280 Gordon Road
Matawan, New Jersey 07747

National Model Railroad Assoc.
4121 Cromwell Road
Chattonooga, Tn. 37421
615-892-2846

Toy Train Operating Society
25 West Walnut Street
Suite 308
Pasadena, Ca. 91103
1-818-578-0673

Train Collectors Association
PO Box 248
Strasburg, Pa. 17579

Train Shows
Great American Train Show
PO Box 1745
Lombard, Ill. 60148
708-834-0652

Greenberg Shows, Inc.
7566 Main Street
Sykesville, Md. 21784
410-795-7447

Northern Jersey Train-O-Rama
c/o Donald Brill
39 6th Street
Dover, New Jersey 07801

St. Vincent DePaul's Train Show
1510 DePaul Street
Elmont, Long Island,
New York 11003
516-352-2127

The Westchester Toy & Train Assoc., Inc.
217-36 50th Ave.
Bayside, New York 11364
1-718-228-6282

York Train Show
c/o Jules Ermel
65 Arbor Road
Cinnaminson, New Jersey 08077
609-829-4222

Vehicles, Structures & Figures
Arttista Accessories
1616 South Franklin Street
Philadelphia, Pa. 19148

Buildings Unlimited
PO Box 239
Nazareth, Pa. 18064

Chapman Creations
3379 Route 46
Intervale Gardens Apt. 10B
Parsippany, NJ. 07054
201-299-8611

Design Preservations
Box 280
Crestone, Co. 81131

Eastwood Automobilia
580 Lancaster Ave.
Malvern, Pa. 19355
215-640-1450

Pioneer Valley Models
PO Box 4928
Holyoke, Ma. 01041

Steam-Era Structures Co.
PO Box 54285
Cincinnati, Ohio 45254

Triple Diamond Replicas Inc.
2211 South Mt. Prospect
Des Plaines, Ill. 60018

Brasilia Press
PO Box 2023
Elkhart, Indiana 46515

Videos
Encore Entertainment
626 South Main
Frankenmuth, Mi. 48734
517-652-8881

Pentrex
2652 East Walnut Street
Pasadena, Ca. 91107
818-793-3400

The Train Station
12 Romaine Road
Mountain Lakes, New Jersey 07046
201-263-1979

TM Books & Video
Box 279
New Buffalo, Michigan 49117
219-879-2822

Video Rails
5076 Santa Fe
San Diego, Ca. 92109
619-581-0303

Additional Information

The *Toy Train Revue* video magazine is devoted to every aspect of toy trains. Each show is a snappy 60 minutes of layouts, collections, interviews, product reviews, operating tips, and factory tours – a great mix of toy train action, how-to's, and commentary.

Produced by well known toy train video producer, Tom McComas, the *Toy Train Revue* video magazine is both entertaining and informative. It may be purchased by subscription or individually, as each issue is released.
To order, call 1-800-892-2822

The *Toy Train Revue Journal* is a market report, tip sheet, and price guide all rolled into one quarterly magazine – the essential companion for the toy train collector and operator.

Our hobby has changed dramatically over the past few years and not all the changes have been for the good. Unscrupulous practices, like selling fakes and reproductions as originals, are costing innocent collectors thousands of dollars. The *Toy Train Revue Journal* addresses these issues and others which are crucial to the growth of the hobby.

The *TTRJ* also contains articles on collecting and operating toy trains, what's hot and what's not, and price guide updates. It is current, relevant, and necessary, ideal for both the beginner and seasoned collector.
To order, call 1-800-892-2822.

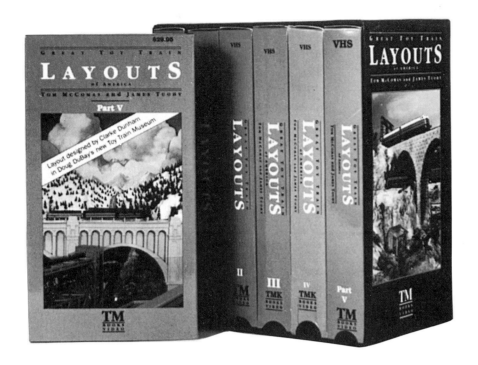

This six-part video series is an in-depth study of the most elaborate model train layouts in America. Almost six hours of action plus interviews with the layout builders. Trains and accessories of every era and almost every manufacturer. Each 45 to 55 minute show is filled with tips and hints and insights on how the experts build layouts.

Part two was chosen by *People Magazine* as one of the ten best videos of the year. If you are thinking about building a layout, or just enjoy good stories about toy trains and the people who love them, this series is a must. **To order call 1-800-892-2822.**

A delightful and innovative video. Thirty minutes of toy trains, real trains, real animals, kids singing, rockets to the moon, fireworks – even a brief appeal for environmental awareness. Fast-paced action that will keep your kids (and older kids, too) enchanted time and time again.

This video is a marvelous way to introduce your kids to the fun and excitement of toy trains. They will laugh, they will learn and they will want to watch it again.

"Pure joy from beginning to end. Real trains, cows, little trains, Ward Kimball, lions – great original music. All creatures great and small should have a copy of this video."
Bruce Manson, *Train Collectors Quarterly*

"I Love Toy Trains replaced *Thomas The Tank* as my kid's favorite video. Best babysitter in town."
Michael Salnick, Palm Beach, Fla.

To order or for a free catalog, call 1-800-892-2822